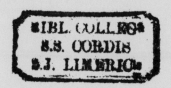

D1421186

The Viking World

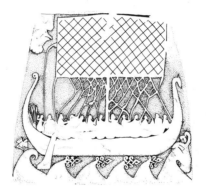

The Viking World

Jacqueline Simpson

B T Batsford Ltd   London

FRONTISPIECE
Plain helmet with nose-guard;
eleventh-century bone-carving
from Sigtuna, Sweden.

This edition first published 1980

Text © Jacqueline Simpson, 1967, 1980
ISBN 0 7134 0777 8

Filmset in Monophoto Ehrhardt by
Servis Filmsetting Ltd, Manchester
Printed and bound in Great Britain by
Butler & Tanner Ltd, Frome, Somerset
for the Publishers
B.T. Batsford Ltd, 4 Fitzhardinge Street,
London WIH OAH

Contents

Illustrations and Provenances

8

Acknowledgment

The Author and Publishers thank the following for their kind permission to reproduce copyright illustrations. The Publishers apologise if they have unwittingly omitted to acknowledge any sources or made incorrect attributions.
Antiquarian Topographical Archives, Stockholm – 15, 16, 20, 35, 80, 93 (2), 130 (2), 138, 148 (B), 152 (2), 155, 156, 162. Arnamagnian Institute, Copenhagen – 88, 140, 184 (T). A Binns – 14. Icelandic Photo and Press Service – 47. Loftleidir Icelandic Photo (nr 7007-146-2) – 143. Manx Museum, 25 (2). Museum of London 119 (B). National Museum of Antiquities, Copenhagen – 24, 58, 106, 125 (2), 134, 135, 150, 177. National Museum of Antiquities, Scotland, 19, 27 (2). National Museum of Iceland, 12, 53, 163, 174. National Museum of Ireland, 23 (2). National Museum of Schleswig Holstein, 89, 90, 117. Oxford University Institute of Archaeology, 139. State History Museum, Stockholm – frontispiece, 4 (Lars Bergström), 55 (2), 34, 99, 111, 146, 147, 165, 167, 172. University Museum of National Antiquities, Oslo – 50, 51, 56, 60 (2), 61, 66, 67, 68, 70, 71, 72, 75, 76 (2), 99, 103, 107, 112, 115 (2), 119 (T), 120, 158. Viking Ship Museum – Roskilde, Denmark, 78. York Archaeological Trust – (Mike Duffy), 62. and Mrs Eva Wilson for the line drawings.

1
Ruffians or Heroes?

In medieval Scandinavian languages, a *vikingr* is a pirate, a freebooter who seeks wealth either by ship-borne raids on foreign coasts or by waylaying more peaceful seafarers in home waters. There is also an abstract noun *viking*, meaning 'the act of going raiding overseas'; the word is used in this sense in the quotation on p. 64. Strictly speaking, therefore, the term Viking should only be applied to men actually engaged in these violent pursuits, and not to every contemporary Scandinavian farmer, merchant, settler or craftsman, nor even to warriors fighting in the dynastic wars of their lords or in their own private feuds. However, it was the raiders who made the most impact on the Europe of their time, and who have attracted most attention among historians since, so that it has become customary to apply the term 'Viking Age' to the period of Scandinavian history beginning in the 790s (the time of the first recorded raids on western Europe) and petering out somewhere round the middle of the eleventh century (by which time raids and emigrations had ceased, the settlements established abroad had become thoroughly integrated with the local populations, and social changes in the Scandinavian homelands had marked the transition to their true Middle Ages). Indeed, the term is such a convenient label for the distinctive culture of this period that one now talks not only of 'Viking ships' and 'Viking weapons' but of 'Viking art', 'Viking houses', and even 'Viking agriculture' – expressions which would have seemed meaningless to people living at the time.

Nor were the Viking raiders as a whole referred to by that name by their contemporaries. The Anglo-Saxons called them all 'Danes', whichever land they came from; the Franks called them *Normanni*, 'Northmen'; the Germans called them 'Ashmen', perhaps in allusion to their ships, though these were in fact made of oak; the Irish called them either *Gaill*, 'Foreigners', or *Lochlannaigh*, 'Northerners', though they also sometimes distinguished between Danes and Norwegians as 'Black Northerners' and 'White Northerners'; Spanish Arabs called them *Majus*, 'Heathens'; in the east, the Slavs, Arabs and Byzantine Greeks called them *Rus* or *Ros*, which probably was originally a Finnish name for the Swedes. As for the Scandinavians themselves, they usually thought of themselves as inhabitants of a particular region – 'Men of Vestfold', 'Men of Hordaland', 'Men of the Uplands', and so forth – but as the sense of national identity grew so too did the use of national names. They also used the term *Nordmenn*, sometimes in the limited sense 'Norwegians' but more often in the general sense 'Scandinavians'; the latter usage has given rise to the terms 'Northmen', 'Norsemen' and 'Norse' in modern English. As for the word *vikingr*, its origins are obscure and have been much debated; probably the most widely accepted suggestion is that it comes from '*vik*', 'a creek, bay, or fjord', and arose because sea-raiders tend to lurk in bays and river mouths in order to waylay passing ships, and to have a base for raids along the coast.

Discussion of the Viking Age has all too often been dominated by a picture of fierce, pitiless barbarians spreading terror and destruction in their boundless lust for loot, and many less sensational but equally important aspects of the period have been overlooked. This is largely due to the one-sided view presented by contemporary European chroniclers who, very understandably, saw the Vikings solely as plunderers and extorters of tribute; such writers knew little and cared less about their background, their culture, their trade, or even the underlying reasons for their coming. However accurate the actual facts in a chronicle may be, its overall picture will be distorted, both by emotional bias and by the omission of other facts which the chronicler either did not know or did not think worth recording. Even the *Anglo-Saxon Chronicle*, which is far fuller and better informed than most such records, is almost exclusively concerned with military campaigns; it spares only one or two casual sentences for the actual settlement of the Danelaw, which was going on at the same period and had far more complex and long-lasting social consequences. Often a close study of place-names and linguistic evidence is the only way to fill out the gaps in contemporary writings.

Later medieval writers are often still more violently partisan in their accounts. The author of the twelfth-century Irish text *The War of the*

Stone from Lindisfarne Priory, showing Viking raiders.

Gaedhil with the Gaill (i.e. of the Irishmen against the Vikings), looking back to the horrors of the Viking attacks, which had evidently not grown less in the telling, exclaims:

> In a word, although there were an hundred hard, steeled, iron heads on one neck, and an hundred sharp, ready, cool, never-rusting, brazen tongues in each head, and an hundred garrulous, loud, unceasing voices from each tongue, they could not recount, or narrate, or enumerate, or tell what all the Gaedhil suffered in common, both men and women, laity and clergy, old and young, noble and ignoble, of hardship, and of injury, and of oppression, in every house, from these valiant, wrathful, foreign, purely-pagan people.

Modern historians have of course realized the bias and exaggerations in medieval sources, yet their own judgments are sometimes hardly less emotional. As late as 1930 Sir Thomas Kendrick, while conceding that some Viking settlers took land peacefully, nevertheless repeatedly used such phrases as 'brutish barbarians', 'ruffian robbers', 'pests who plagued the outer fringes of the civilized world', 'bloodthirsty and abominable barbarians, enemies of society capable of infamous, indefensible outrages of arson and slaughter'. The only thing he could find to praise in them was their craftsmanship, of which he remarked that 'no one who has ever looked at the [Oseberg] ship herself . . . can ever again think of the ninth-century Norsemen as completely vile and soulless barbarians'.

Many books on the Viking Age contain similar judgements, though perhaps less strongly worded. However, there exists a very different school of thought, chiefly among students of Norse literature rather than of European history. Basing themselves on the heroic Scandinavian poetry and the Icelandic prose sagas, these scholars built up a highly favourable picture of the Vikings and their way of life, seeing them as models of all the manly virtues – courage, hardihood, loyalty, love of individual freedom, and a sense of honour. The literary sources do indeed present many heroes thoroughly imbued with these qualities, which were clearly much admired in the Nordic world, and at the same time it is true that the actual historical achievements of the Vikings presupposed great courage and enterprise. Certain authors have carried their admiration for the Vikings so far as to ascribe all the virtues of the English character to the presence among our ancestors of those whom R.L. Bremmer (in 1923) called:

> a race of hardy folk, men and women of simple and heroic mould. Their bodies were strong, well built and shapely, their features for the most part comely, and often of classic beauty. Their manners were direct and homely, their minds responsive to all the finer human emotions – love, chivalry, courage, freedom, and justice. . . . [Men] ready to be outspoken and merry in any company, true to a trust, slow to wrath, fearless in fight and steadfast in friendship. . . . These three great virtues – honour, chivalry and love of freedom – are part of the deathless inheritance we have received from our Northern forefathers.

This glowing picture, as has been remarked already, is mainly based on information gleaned from Norse literature, but this, though in many ways offering extremely valuable insights into Scandinavian mentality, has dangers of its own for the historian who follows it too uncritically. It is only the poetry which actually dates back to the Viking Age, and much of this (with its emphasis on warlike prowess, loyalty, honour, generosity, and unflinching courage in the face of doom) expresses the ideals of heroic conduct admired among aristocrats and their warrior followers – ideals which were not directly relevant to the daily preoccupations of a farmer or a merchant, even if they might inspire him in moments of peril. The fact that such legendary heroes as Sigurd the Volsung were ever-popular subjects for poetry and art does not mean that every Viking aspired to be a Sigurd.

As for the Icelandic sagas, these are in many ways the most fascinating sources available, but their apparent objectivity and sober, realistic tone conceal many pitfalls. None of them was written before the twelfth century, and most of the finest and best known were composed when the thirteenth was well advanced. Those of most value to the historian fall into two groups: biographies and other factual writings, notably lives of Norwegian kings and accounts of the early history of Iceland itself; and the 'Family Sagas', which

Nineteenth-century Icelanders listening to sagas: painting by H.A.G. Schiott, *c.*1860.

describe the lives and especially the feuds of individual Icelanders living in the tenth and early eleventh centuries. Sagas of the first type were meant as factual history, even if they sometimes fell into inaccuracies or incorporated legendary material; but the Family Sagas were artistic interpretations of the past, so that the kernel of tradition round which they were built may have become distorted. The men who composed them were often eager antiquarians, making use of every scrap of information to bridge the 200-year gap between themselves and their subject-matter; yet the very fact that they were so fascinated by former centuries makes one wonder how far they idealized the past. Certainly they over-simplified it; for instance, they often ascribed the settlement of Iceland solely to the proud anger of Norwegian chieftains whose independence was threatened by Harald Fairhair, when in fact it was part of a far larger movement in which economic pressures were probably decisive. All the same, the sagas, if used critically, are indispensable sources for Scandinavian history. The greatest achievement in strictly historical writing is *Heimskringla*, a superb series of Sagas of the Kings of Norway, composed by Snorri Sturluson in the 1220s; Snorri was also an authority on heathen myths and ancient poetry, and without his work on these subjects our knowledge of Scandinavian religion would be drastically curtailed.

The sagas contain a mass of incidental references to many aspects of daily life – food, clothes, farming, law and much else – which is often of great value in showing, from the inside, the ordinary non-heroic side of Scandinavian life. But here there is always a risk that the writer may have been unconsciously misled by customs of his own time; sometimes the anachronisms are obvious, but often it is only after archaeological evidence has come to light that one can tell what is or is not anachronistic. There is a good example concerning houses. *Grettir's Saga* (quoted on p. 43) explicitly says that Viking Age houses consisted of a single large room where all domestic activities took place; but one Icelandic scholar, convinced that such primitive conditions must have been abandoned by that date, analysed terms used in many other sagas, and concluded that the houses described all contained several rooms with distinct names. Later, archaeological excavations proved that *Grettir's Saga* was right; of other sagas, a few gave definitely inaccurate descriptions influenced by the houses of their own times, while the rest used terms so ambiguous that only the discovery of actual remains could show how they should be interpreted.

Another disadvantage of Family Sagas as sources for the Viking Age is that their outlook is so firmly centred on Iceland itself. If one of their heroes goes abroad, it is just an interlude, perhaps to be dismissed in the briefest terms ('He went to Norway, where the king gave him good welcome'; or 'That summer he sailed for Ireland; for three years he raided there, and returned home with much wealth'); or, if treated more fully, the adventures are of a conventional dramatized type which cast hardly any light on the conditions of the age. There are exceptions, notably *Egil's Saga*, but on the whole the heroes of the Family Sagas play out their destinies at home; these works give a detailed picture of life inside one Scandinavian community, but they have little to say about the interaction between Scandinavia and the rest of Europe.

Shortly after the end of the period come the first written Scandinavian law-codes, set down in the twelfth century. Some of their evidence on such matters as the status of slaves and women and the conduct of lawsuits can safely be applied to the Viking Age, at any rate in its later phases.

Warrior buried with weapons: carved cross, Middleton, North Yorkshire.

The problem of forming a balanced picture of the Vikings from written sources alone is thus extremely thorny, for the European chronicles and the native literature seem almost to be describing a different race of men, and each can be suspected of emotional bias – of seeing enemies through a haze of blood and smoke, or of idealizing ancestors in a golden glow of heroism and high-mindedness. Fortunately, a few contemporaries who came in contact with the Vikings were able to view them more dispassionately, and often it is their brief, casual pieces of information which prove the most illuminating. Ecclesiastical historians describing the work of missionaries incidentally reveal something about conditions of trade or travel, or give a few facts about heathen religion; Arab geographers provide remarkable descriptions of the customs of Swedish traders in Russia; a Byzantine Emperor explains their seasonal movements along the Dnieper trade-route. The world thus revealed is by no means free from violence, but at least the writers are aware of the underlying economic factors, and do not view the Vikings as the inexplicable scourge which they sometimes seemed to the harassed West.

Moreover, archaeology has revealed a wide variety of material remains which provide a mass of evidence, direct and indirect, to help our understanding of the Viking Age. One major source of such remains is the many thousands of graves that have been excavated, for it was a custom of many (but not all) Scandinavians to provide the dead with clothes, weapons, tools and other possessions before burying or cremating them. If soil conditions are favourable, there is much to be learnt from the contents of the graves; they range from one or two simple items to the lavish equipment of princely burial mounds – ships with all their gear, food supplies, cooking vessels, sledges, harness, and many other objects used in the daily life of a wealthy household. The mounds at Gokstad and Oseberg in Norway are deservedly the most famous of these lavish burials, and there will be many references to their contents in the following pages; yet their glamour must not overshadow the countless smaller graves, whose contents are clues to the way of life among the average level of the population.

The excavation of houses is much rarer than that of graves, for the great majority of sites favoured by the Vikings remained in use throughout the Middle Ages and even to the present day; therefore those that were totally abandoned are of particular value to the modern excavator. There are many such in Greenland, where two whole settlements died out in the Middle Ages and their ruins were left untouched by the Eskimos; there is also an Icelandic valley where farms laid waste by a volcano in 1104 were never reinhabited, and some of these date back to the early tenth century; or again, there are Viking Age houses scattered here and there in the Orkneys, Shetlands, Faroes and Hebrides – notably a fine group of buildings at Jarlshof in the Shetlands, sealed off from later disturbance by a layer of drifting sand.

Even more instructive is the excavation of whole towns, with their grave-fields, harbours and defensive earthworks; any account of the Viking Age must be deeply indebted to the scholars who have studied Birka, Hedeby, Kaupang and Helgö. In the last few years there have been important excavations of Viking Age and medieval material in Dublin and York, at

Aerial view of Birka harbour and defences.

Bergen in Norway and at Lund in Sweden. These were first and foremost trading centres, so that objects found there cast light on the economic aspects of Viking communities, showing what goods were imported and exported, and what crafts practised in the towns themselves. The study of such sites is a lengthy business, requiring many seasons of excavation and prolonged analysis, so that there is certainly still further information to be gained even from those already known, quite apart from any that may be explored in the future. Another type of large-scale site, so far only known from Denmark, is the fortified military encampment; there are four of these camps, of which the best known is Trelleborg.

Then there are the hoards of buried silver, well over 1,000 of them, ranging from tiny finds of two or three coins and a few bits of broken ornaments, to great piles weighing 15 lb or more and each made up of several thousand coins, or of heavy rings, or both. This treasure is not found in graves, nor on sites of houses; it was hidden for safety in the open country, often at the foot of a rock or tree, in the side of an old burial mound, or some similar spot which its owner could easily recognize when the time came to dig it up again. If a region is particularly rich in such hoards, it means not only that the inhabitants were wealthy but that they lived in fear of war or piracy, and also that many of them failed to return to reclaim their treasure; as the coins are datable, they will also indicate the period of these troubles. Occasionally silver hoards are almost the only clue to the importance of a region; for instance, the island of Gotland, off the coast of Sweden, is only once mentioned in a written text from the Viking period and its market-towns have not yet been excavated, yet its treasures prove that it was the

Treasure hoard from Buttle parish, Gotland.

wealthiest area of all Scandinavia. Scandinavia produced no silver of her own, and though mints did exist there, specimens of native coinage are not very numerous in the homelands. Almost all coins found are therefore foreign – Arabic, English, Frankish, German – and had come in from abroad in the course of trade, as plunder, as Danegeld, or as the pay of mercenaries; their quantity and place of origin are vital clues to Viking contacts with the outer world.

The new technique of underwater archaeology has led to the recovery of five Viking ships at Skuldelev, on the Roskilde Fjord in Denmark; two more are known to lie in the sea off Hedeby, but have not yet been salvaged. Another novelty, tree-ring dating (dendrochronology), will eventually enable more precise datings of wooden structures to be made; already it has forced a change in the previously accepted chronology of the Danevirke fortifications and the Trelleborg camp.

Finally, mention must be made of the carved or inscribed stones set up as memorials to the dead, not over their graves, but in some place where they would be seen by many passers-by – beside a ford, along the track of ancient roads, or at an assembly-place. They occur in many parts of Scandinavia, but two areas and periods are particularly rich in them. The first is Gotland in the ninth century (or perhaps the eighth, for the date is in dispute), which produced fine pictorial designs including many human figures. These show battles, processions, ships in full sail, men on horseback; their meaning is often mysterious, but they are very valuable sources for studying the appearance of men and women, since the realistic representation of human figures is extremely rare in Viking art. The second group is from Sweden in the eleventh century; here pictures are few, but ornamental inscriptions give the name of the dead man and of the mourner who had the monument erected, often adding a few details such as the personal qualities of the dead man, his standing in life, and the place and circumstances of his death. Such information can contribute to our understanding of Viking society, though it only occasionally adds a new fact to our historical knowledge.

Through all these varied types of evidence we can examine many facets of the Viking Age. There are of course gaps in our knowledge, and also matters which remain controversial; in dealing with these I have tried to make clear whether a particular interpretation is widely accepted, or whether it is only one among several equally plausible alternatives. The aim of this book is to present the Vikings neither as bloodthirsty ruffians nor as blond, blue-eyed heroes, but to relate their activities to what is known of the material background of their lives. The society which emerges is different from the rest of Europe, and in some ways perhaps more archaic, but it is not one which can reasonably be called primitive, unorganized, or exceptionally cruel.

2
The Expansion of the Vikings

The idea of a 'Viking Age' beginning abruptly in the 790s makes sense from the point of view of Western Europe, but it is important to realize that, from that of the Scandinavians themselves, such a dividing line can only be arbitrary. All the activities one thinks of as characteristic of the Viking Age – raids, piracy, far-flung commerce, colonization of foreign lands – were aspects of a continuous process of expansion, originating now in one part of Scandinavia, now in another, and going right back through the eighth century or even beyond. The difference is that the expansions of the earlier period took place in regions that have left no written records, so that they can only be studied piecemeal by archaeological research; later movements, by contrast, affected the highly literate societies of Western Europe, and so were amply chronicled. Indeed, from about 800 onwards, the documentary sources for Viking raids and campaigns and for the political history of Scandinavia itself become extremely rich, and it is possible to trace the careers of many individual leaders and the movements of military forces in considerable detail; this chapter, however, can only attempt a brief generalized sketch of the main lines of Viking expansion.

The first Scandinavians to become active abroad were the peoples of Sweden and the Baltic island of Gotland, who even in the eighth century were amassing wealth as traders and importing European glass and woollen fabrics, possibly in exchange for iron ore. An important site from the fifth century to the eighth was the island of Helgö in Lake Mälar (Sweden), where there were many buildings forming a centre of trade and craftsmanship; among objects found there is a superb Irish crozier, perhaps booty from some very early Viking raid, and a little Buddha, a sign of Sweden's trade-links with the East. The wealth of Swedish grave-goods at this period confirms the impression of flourishing trade and foreign contacts, while the hoards of buried silver found in Gotland not only prove its prosperity but suggest that its inhabitants often needed to hide their riches from would-be plunderers – presumably raiders from poorer areas of Scandinavia.

Both Swedes and Gotlanders had already begun to expand beyond their native regions well before 700, setting up colonies across the Baltic in what are now Latvia, Lithuania and Estonia, and possibly in Finland too. Particularly important settlements have been revealed by excavations of grave-fields at Grobin (near Libau in Latvia); here there was a community

Cloak pin from Westness, Ronsay.

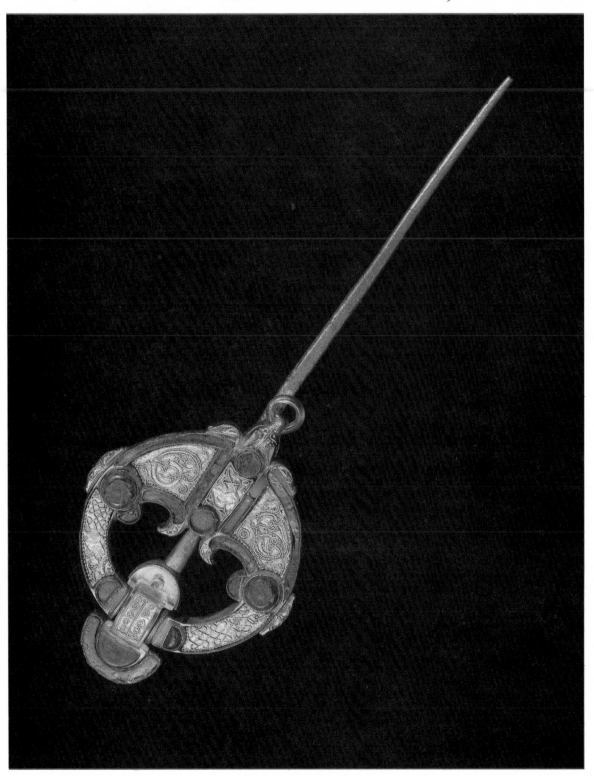

Irish crozier found at Helgö.

of Gotlanders, apparently rich traders accompanied by their women, and also one of Swedes, where there were only men with warriors' gear. A similar colony of Gotland traders existed near Elbing. All this activity around the Baltic coasts is like that of the Viking Age proper, but preceded it by three or four generations; moreover, it led by natural and unbroken development to the ninth-century Swedish expansion along the waterways of Russia – a movement which was primarily a quest for new trade-routes, and will be discussed in Chapter 5.

At the end of the eighth century, it was the Norwegians who were on the move, and Western Europe reacted with alarm to the news of their attacks. The first of these to be recorded may have been an incident on the Dorset coast in the reign of Beorhtric of Wessex (786–802), when three ship-loads of Norwegians killed the reeve who tried to bring them by force to the king's court. Or the first raid may have been the far more famous attack on Lindisfarne in 793, when heathen men landed on the island, slaughtered cattle to re-stock their ships, plundered the monastery, and killed several monks and nuns. The horror felt by Christians at this outrage increased during the next few years as further raids were made on Scotland, Ireland, Wales and northern England, many of them involving pillaging of monasteries and shrines.

Contemporaries saw these raids simply as wanton looting of Church treasures, and indeed this was obviously the reason for these particular incidents. Yet they were only part of a far larger pattern of Norwegian activity, directed chiefly towards the islands north and west of Scotland, in which the main motive was almost certainly an urgent search for fresh lands to settle – for by this time the Norwegians, penned between the mountains and the sea, had made use of all the land at their disposal, and were possibly also suffering from a rapid rise in population. There was, it is true, a strong tradition of piracy in Norway, where coastal chieftains often lived by preying on passing merchant ships, and it is obvious that once such men discovered rich Western churches and monasteries virtually undefended, they would not be slow to profit from them; nevertheless, the main story of Norwegian expansion is one of colonizing.

By about 800, Norwegians were establishing themselves on the Orkneys and Shetlands, and shortly afterwards Irish hermits left the Faroes 'because of robber Northmen'. Viking graves from the first half of the ninth century are common on the Orkneys, especially on Westray; Viking houses have been excavated at Birsay, Buckquoy and Aikerness in the Orkneys and at Jarlshof in the Shetlands, the latter being thought to be an early ninth-century settlement. Other farmhouses of similarly early date have been excavated on the Shetland island of Unst, and at Kvivik on the Faroe island of Streymoy. There can be little doubt that the colonization of all these islands began about 800 and continued intermittently over the next 100 years. The settlers chiefly lived by farming, fishing and seal-hunting, though at the same time they must certainly have profited from their excellent situation for trading and raiding further south. Some certainly were rich; the grave of a woman with lavish jewellery was found at Westness on Ronsay in 1963, while as long ago as 1858 an exceptionally rich hoard of silver neck-rings, arm-rings and brooches was unearthed at Skaill Bay.

The Faroes were empty when the Norwegians came, save for the Irish hermits who fled from them, and it has sometimes been argued that the same must have been true of the Orkneys and Shetlands, the Picts having declined almost to the point of extinction, and that the settlement was therefore a wholly peaceful affair. Yet the evidence of archaeology and place-name study increasingly contradicts this theory; it seems likely that a thirteenth-century Norwegian history is right in saying that Vikings found both Picts and Irish-Scottish priests on these islands – though it must be mistaken in adding that they slaughtered them all. Among the earliest buildings at Jarlshof there is one built to a Norse plan but with the masonry technique of the pre-Norse inhabitants, and containing their characteristic slate and stone tools; evidently here the Norwegian settler kept dispossessed Picts working as his slaves. A site at Buckquoy (Orkney) excavated in 1970/1 reveals a more fruitful integration of the two cultures – first a Pictish house whose builders had adopted Norse architectural techniques, then some fifty years later a Norse house whose inhabitants used Pictish-style pins, combs and pottery. There may have been some looting in these regions, for the discovery of a hoard of Celtic silver on St Ninian's Isle in 1958 strongly suggests that the Christian Picts of Shetland were more prosperous than had been hitherto supposed; however, the islands were not merely raided, but colonized by a flow of Norwegian migrants so numerous that the language and place-names, and also the legal and taxation systems, became overwhelmingly and permanently Scandinavian.

During the early ninth century the plundering of Ireland increased in scale and frequency, until in 820, according to the *Annals of Ulster*, 'the ocean poured such torrents of foreigners over Erin that there was no harbour or landing-place, fortress or stronghold, without fleets of Vikings and pirates'. In 836 the first Viking settlement was founded in Dublin, and in 839 there arrived a certain Turgeis, who set up his headquarters at Armagh, the chief Christian see, and was acknowledged 'king of all the foreigners in Erin'; his wife had her residence at the monastery of Clonmacnoise, where she, as heathen priestess, gave oracles from the altar. Irish men and women were seized as slaves, sometimes for sale and sometimes as labour for the new settlements, especially Iceland. Wealthy Christian centres were, naturally, looted; not surprisingly, the loot has left many traces in Viking graves – bronze mountings from book-bindings, reliquaries or caskets, torn off and roughly adapted as brooches; or, occasionally, entire objects of a religious nature, such as a reliquary, obviously a keepsake from the plundering of an Irish church. The vast majority of such things have been found in Norway, or in Norwegian graves in Scotland and Ireland itself; only two or three have been found in Denmark and Sweden, showing that these two countries played hardly any part in this phase of the attack on Ireland.

OPPOSITE
Bronze disc brooch from Dublin.

Carved bone trial-piece from Dublin.

It is not clear whether the Vikings made any serious attempt to settle the Irish countryside. However, they unquestionably made a major impact on Ireland by creating fortified harbours which soon grew into flourishing towns, centres of trade and craftsmanship well placed for contact with Britain, western France and Spain, as well as Scandinavia itself. Dublin, Wexford, Cork and Limerick all began in this way. In the last ten years, archaeology has revealed a great deal about the Viking period in Dublin's history, especially its commercial activities in the tenth and eleventh centuries. Among the many houses uncovered, several were workshops producing objects carved from the antlers of Irish red deer: combs in vast numbers (300 have been found already), comb-cases, whistles, knife-handles, pins, toggles, gaming pieces, chessmen. There were also bone 'trial-pieces' on which craftsmen practised patterns that would then be translated into metalwork. Other buildings housed woodworkers making lathe-turned dishes, bowls and trays; others, metalworkers producing (among other items) amulets of Thor's Hammer and bronze pins – over 700 of the latter have been found. There was also a shipwright's yard. Besides this vigorous export trade in craft objects, it has been suggested that Irish towns served as centres for a slave-trade aimed at the Arabs of Spain and North Africa.

The relation of the Vikings to the Irish themselves remains more obscure, though their presence must have indirectly affected the local economy – for instance, people must have been paid to gather up the huge numbers of shed antlers that were needed for the Dublin bone-carving industry. It is also

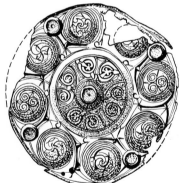

Irish book-mount found in Norway.

Irish reliquary found in Norway.

known that Viking warriors hired themselves out as mercenaries to various Irish kings, and thus became a factor in local politics. The Irish chronicles tell a tangled tale of warfare between Norwegians and Irish, complicated by internal rivalries and shifting alliances; and towards the middle of the century there was ferocious fighting between the established Norwegians and the newly arriving Danes. Ireland also served as a starting-point for fresh expeditions which, by the end of the century, had led to the colonization of the Isle of Man and of many areas of south-west Scotland, Cumberland, Westmorland, Lancashire and Cheshire. It is also likely that many of the raiding bands that harassed England and Wales had made use of Irish ports as their bases.

The Isle of Man is an area of particular interest, because its art so clearly demonstrates the blending of Norse and Celtic culture, and also because it has preserved to this day many Scandinavian features in law and administration. The settlers here seem to have been simply prosperous farmers attracted by 'the best land in the Southern Isles' (i.e. in the Hebrides, of which Man was reckoned one); there is no sign of a trading-centre. They apparently lived peacefully among a Celtic population, with whom they soon intermarried, and by whom they were converted. This mixture of cultures produced a series of noble monuments – the Manx stone crosses of the tenth century. Their shape (a slab incised with a wheel-headed cross) is Scottish; their inscriptions are Norse, carved in runes; of the names mentioned on them, 44 are Norse, 22 Irish and 1 Pictish. The artist who introduced the style was a Norseman named Gaut; his finest work is

A missionary saint: Kirk Andreas Cross, Isle of Man. Odin and the wolf: Kirk Andreas Cross, Isle of Man.

probably the Kirk Michael cross, made for a Celtic patron, but he also worked for Scandinavians. He flourished in the period 930–950. The ornamentation on these crosses includes both Celtic and Scandinavian types of interlacing bands, and also human and animal figures. Some of these represent scenes from Norse mythology and heroic legends. It is most remarkable (though not unique to Man) that heathen themes should decorate Christian monuments; sometimes a deliberate contrast seems intended, as at Kirk Andreas, where Odin dragged down to destruction by the wolf is balanced by a Christian figure triumphantly trampling on the serpent of evil. The Norwegian colonies in Cumberland and Westmorland also produced sculpture of similar intention, notably the Gosforth Cross with its contrasted scenes of the Crucifixion and of the Doom of the Gods.

Norse colonies in Scotland and the Isles must have contained a similar fusion of races and cultures. One telling example of this is the brooch found at Hunterston on the Ayrshire coast; this superb piece of Scottish Celtic craftsmanship bears on the reverse side a Norse inscription in runes, recording that 'Melbrigda owns this brooch' – 'Melbrigda' being a Celtic name, though both language and lettering are Norse. There was intermarriage in the upper levels of the two societies, to judge from the occurrence of Celtic names in the families of Norse Hebridean chieftains; many households must also have had Celtic slaves, though these would not necessarily be local people, since captives from Ireland were sold far and wide.

In about 860, Iceland, already a refuge for a few wandering Irish hermits, was discovered by Scandinavians. One account says the first to sight it was a Norwegian, Naddod the Viking, blown off course on his way to the Faroes; others, that it was a Swede named Gardar, similarly storm-driven when sailing to the Hebrides. The first to attempt real settlement was the Norwegian Floki and his companions, but they failed through lack of foresight:

> The whole fjord was full of fish and seals, and because of the fishing they overlooked the need to make hay, and their livestock died during the winter. Spring was very cold. Floki walked north to a mountain and saw a fjord full of drift-ice, so they named the land Iceland. . . . Next summer they sailed for Norway. Floki gave the land a bad name, Herjolf had both good and bad to say of it, while Thorolf swore that butter dripped from every blade of grass in the land they had found, and for this reason he was nicknamed Thorolf Butter.

In the following decade – the traditional date is 874 – settlement was begun in earnest by two Norwegian foster-brothers, Ingolf and Leif, who sailed in two ships with their followers and womenfolk, their livestock, and some captured Irish slaves. Leif was killed by his slaves, but Ingolf's settlement prospered, and many men followed his example. Detailed traditions about the settlers were preserved among their descendants, and eventually recorded in the great twelfth-century *Landnamabók*, 'The Book of

Celtic brooch from Hunterston, Scotland.

Reverse side of Hunterston brooch, showing runic inscription.

the Land-Takings'; this preserves the names of some 400 leading men and over 3,000 of their followers, families and slaves, describes where they settled, and outlines their adventures. The process of colonization lasted about 60 years, and it has been reckoned that when it was complete the population must have been close on 20,000.

The settlers came in groups whose leader was usually already a chieftain, or at least of good birth. These leaders staked a claim to large tracts of land, lighting beacons or setting up boundary marks, and spent some time exploring their chosen region before setting up a permanent farmstead. The process is well described in the thirteenth-century *Egil's Saga*, which tells how a certain Skallagrim took land in Borgarfjord. First he explored, finding that 'there were great marshes there, and broad woodlands, with much space between the mountains and the sea; there was ample seal-hunting, and good fishing'. Then he laid claim to a huge area, and chose for his own farm a certain spot where the coffin of his dead father had been washed ashore after he threw it overboard for an omen. The rest of his area he parcelled out among the various kinsmen and dependants who had sailed with him from Norway, so that they could set up their own farmsteads. Such land was always held as freehold, with no question of tenancy or feudal dues, the former being rare and the latter unknown in Viking Age society. Eventually the settlers would live by their sheep and cattle, but in the early years foraging was very necessary. *Egil's Saga* says:

> Skallagrim was a very hard-working man; he always kept many men about him, and often sent them to seek whatever provisions were to be found there and might serve to support men, for at first they had little livestock compared with what was needed for the number of men there were there; but what livestock there was roamed the woods all winter, foraging for itself. Skallagrim was a great ship-builder, and there was no shortage of driftwood west of Myrar. . . . He sent men out rowing for fish, and seal-hunting, and egg-gathering, for at that time there were plenty of all such provisions, and also driftwood to be brought in. At that time too there were many whales stranded, and whoever wished to spear them could do so. All the hunting-grounds there were undisturbed, for man had been unknown.

Most settlers came from western Norway, where the pressure of population and the land-shortage were most acute. Yet such a mundane explanation of the great exodus found no place in the traditions of the Icelanders, who preferred to think that their ancestors had come from more dramatic motives – because of blood-feuds and outlawries, or because they opposed Harald Fairhair's policy of uniting the petty Norwegian kingships under his own rule. Such factors may well have influenced a few famous leaders, but the movement as a whole must have had far deeper roots.

Nor was it only from Norway that men came; there were some Swedes and Danes too, and, according to *Landnamabók*, almost 12 per cent came from the Norwegian colonies in the British Isles. Men from these areas can hardly have been much affected by the policies of Harald Fairhair; they must simply have felt attracted by a land of ample pastures unencumbered by any native population – for the Irish hermits soon left Iceland, 'as they were not willing to live beside heathen men'. The colonists who transferred their homes from Ireland, the Hebrides, and other Celtic regions seem to have affected the racial characteristics of the Icelanders, some of them being themselves of mixed Norse and Celtic blood, while others brought Celtic slaves and women with them. It has been suggested that modern Icelandic blood-groups are more like those of northern and western Britain than those of Norway, and that medieval Icelandic skulls also tend to be short, like those of Celts; it is in any case certain that Celtic names were fairly common in Iceland at all levels of society. Yet the Icelanders always felt themselves to have strong links with Norway, which they regarded almost as a second homeland; the colonization of Iceland represents the most permanent outcome – though by no means the furthest limit – of the expansion of men of Norwegian stock.

Meanwhile, Danish raids and invasions had been spreading consternation through France and England, their major onslaughts having begun in the 830s and 840s. Thanks to contemporary chroniclers, the detailed course of these attacks can be studied in any history of the period; yet, paradoxically, they are in some ways harder to understand than the less well documented story of the Norwegian colonies. The central puzzle is the motive of these Danish Vikings. Were they simply seeking easy wealth, either by looting or by demanding Danegeld? And what did they do with the money, since only 125 ninth-century coins from England or the Frankish empire have been found in all Scandinavia, despite the heavy payments of Danegeld mentioned by the chroniclers? It has recently been argued that even at this period many of the raiders were primarily interested in finding new land, and that their plundering was merely a way of winning enough wealth to set themselves up as farmers. It may well be that all the emphasis on looting and ravaging is somewhat misleading, and that even during the first decades of the raids a good deal of settlement was going on, unnoticed by the chroniclers.

Certainly by the 870s settlement had become a major preoccupation of the Danes in England, and the famous treaty by which Alfred recognized much of northern and eastern England as Danish territory was simply giving legal basis to what was largely an accomplished fact. Already in 876 one group of Danish fighting-men had withdrawn from the campaign and had 'shared out the land of the Northumbrians and begun to plough it', and another group 'rebuilt the city of York, cultivated the land in its neighbourhood and settled there'; next year others did the same in Mercia, and others in 880 in East Anglia; finally, in 896, 'the Danish army divided, one part going into East Anglia and the other into Northumbria, and those that were moneyless got ships and went south across the sea to the Seine'. Allusions in the *Anglo-Saxon Chronicle* show that these areas were organized on military lines, with key towns as strongholds, and with local levies of Danes sallying forth at intervals to raid the English kingdoms. One might easily assume that the actual settlement was brought about by violence, with Danes driving Englishmen out of their farms and villages by main force – yet there is evidence that this was far from being the case.

The most important single clue to the study of the Danelaw is its place-names – not just names of towns and villages, but of parishes, fields and woods. Difficulties of interpretation can arise, since one must try to distinguish between names given by ninth-century settlers and others given by their descendants over several generations, but the main picture is quite clear. First, as is seen from Professor A.H. Smith's map of Scandinavian parish names, the line agreed on in Alfred and Guthrum's treaty did indeed form a real boundary. Secondly, a thick cluster of names in the north-west reveals a settlement which passes quite unmentioned by any English document, but which we know from Irish sources was due to a movement of Norwegians across the Irish Sea. The date and circumstances of the settlement in west Wales are more conjectural; many of the place-names concerned refer to islands and headlands which served as sailors' landmarks. However, clusters of names near Fishguard and Milford Haven suggest settlement in these areas, possibly by Vikings from Ireland or the Isle of Man.

The most revealing results are reached when one examines the place-names of a particular district side by side with English ones of the same area, taking geographical factors into account. It then appears that Anglo-Saxons were living in considerable numbers even when Scandinavian settlement was thickest, and, what is more, that they lived undisturbed on the sites they had always occupied, while the Scandinavians set about clearing land which the English had not exploited. There was of course much virgin soil still to be found, but it was not necessarily as fertile or well-sited as that already cultivated; nevertheless, both Danes and Norwegians were often content with remote or relatively unattractive holdings – up tributaries rather than main valleys, on the exposed face of hillsides, on the verge of thick woodland, on less fertile or less workable soils, or on comparatively small patches of good land, while the English worked the larger patches. Admittedly there were also cases (though probably fewer than is sometimes said) when Danes took over an existing village and renamed it in their own tongue – though even so this need not mean that they drove the English inhabitants away. By and large, the Scandinavian settlement (as distinct from the campaigns preceding it) seems to have been a peaceable affair, carried out without much upheaval. The Danes readily adopted the English open-field system of agriculture, while in the north-west the Norwegians took to the uplands, where they went in for sheep-rearing as they had done in their homelands, and thus never came into direct competition with the English.

Though the study of place-names is most informative, it leaves open the question of the precise numbers of the settlers, as there is no means of telling how many households made up the original nucleus of a Danish-named

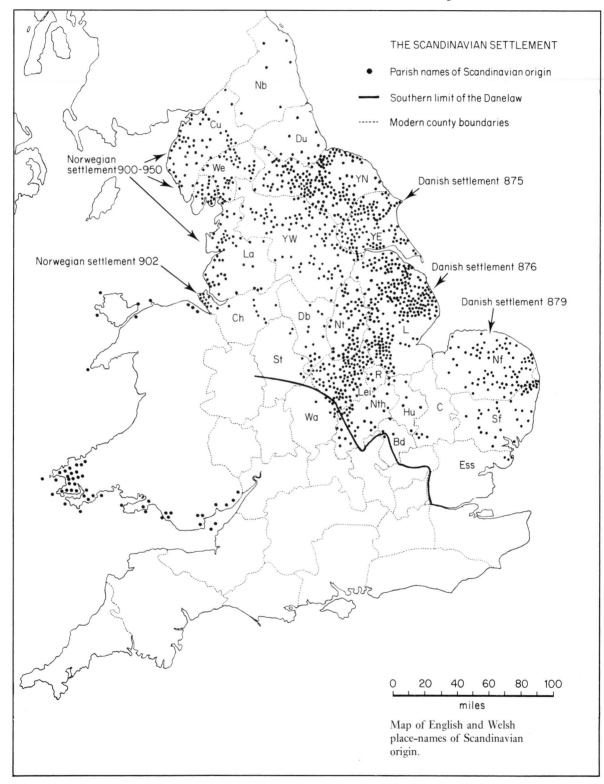

THE SCANDINAVIAN SETTLEMENT

● Parish names of Scandinavian origin

━━━ Southern limit of the Danelaw

···· Modern county boundaries

Norwegian settlement 900-950

Norwegian settlement 902

Danish settlement 875

Danish settlement 876

Danish settlement 879

Nb

Cu

We

Du

YN

YE

YW

La

Ch

Db

Nt

L

St

Wa

Lei

R

Nf

Nth

Hu

C

Sf

Bd

Ess

0   20   40   60   80   100
miles

Map of English and Welsh
place-names of Scandinavian
origin.

village. Here the linguistic evidence is very important, for it shows a deep and permanent Scandinavian influence on the dialects of eastern and northern England, not only by the introduction of many new words, but by affecting pronunciation, grammar and syntax. Much of this influence can be traced in modern Standard English; still more can be seen, even nowadays, in local dialects. It strongly suggests that Scandinavians settled in very great numbers; a small but powerful military aristocracy might account for the adoption of Scandinavian law, but only a mass movement, with interpenetration at all levels of society, could produce so marked a change in the everyday speech of the receiving areas.

Other signs point, though perhaps less conclusively, in the same direction: Scandinavian personal names were popular in these areas even as late as the twelfth century; technical Scandinavian legal terms were widely adopted; the Danelaw system of land measurement and assessment differed from the English; in many parts of the Danelaw there existed, at the time of Domesday Book, very many 'sokemen' – land-owning peasants, considerably more independent of their overlord than men living under the manorial system elsewhere in England – whose status was much like that of small farmers in Scandinavia, and may reflect conditions established by the Danish settlers.

Until recently it had been assumed that the Danish armies campaigning in England in the ninth century were large bodies, probably to be reckoned in thousands, and that the settlement was simply a matter of these men taking their portions of land and perhaps summoning their immediate families to join them. But in the last few years strong arguments have been brought forward for supposing that the armies were far smaller, a few hundreds at the most; if this was so, and if one still accepts that the linguistic and place-name evidence for large-scale settlement cannot be explained away, then others besides the actual fighting-men must have taken part in the colonization.

This is indeed what one might expect; armies conquer new territories, set up strongholds and obtain political ascendancy, and then, taking advantage of this protection, new migrants begin to come over in large numbers from the homeland. The fact that English chroniclers say nothing about any such movement matters little. They were not interested in events inside the Danelaw, only in the changing fortunes in the struggle between Danes and Englishmen; the arrival of peaceful settlers would probably not have struck them as worth recording even if they learnt of it, which they almost certainly would not. Proof or disproof of the occurrence of such migrations can only be sought in even closer study of place-names; already it has been shown that certain groups of villages look, from their sites, as if they had been founded by immigrants making their way inland from the Lincolnshire coast and the Humber estuary, rather than by men of the armies fanning out from their headquarters at Lincoln and Nottingham.

The Danes also took control of existing towns and made them into centres of trade and administration to their own advantage. As has already been noted, they are said to have 'rebuilt' York in 876 (which presumably means they restored damaged fortifications), and their kings reigned there from that date till 954; they also took over in Stamford, Derby, Nottingham, Lincoln and Leicester. Their activities can be well studied at York, on the evidence of coinage minted there, local streetnames, and recent excavations. The picture that emerges is of a town of merchants and small-scale craftsmen, living in wooden or wattle houses and practising such trades as bone-carving, leather-work and smithying; the name of one street, Skeldergate, shows it was a centre for shield-makers (Norse *skjaldari*), while another, Coppergate, belonged to coopers (*koppari*). The districts investigated so far have revealed rather second-rate buildings and homely artefacts, apart from one elegantly carved fragment of a chair; but that is just the result of chance, since historical sources make it certain that York was a place of major political and economic importance – 'wealthy beyond words', according to one writer in the late Anglo-Saxon period, because of the riches of merchants who gathered there from all quarters, 'especially from the Danish people'. The other towns of the Danelaw also grew and throve, and there are even indications that Scandinavian merchants lived in London itself and played a part in its increasing commercial importance in the late tenth and eleventh centuries.

The Danes had, of course, other spheres of interest besides England. In the 850s some made a determined effort to establish a foothold in Ireland, in rivalry to the Norwegians already there. The Irish welcomed them with open arms, and in the first two battles the Danes crushingly defeated the Norwegians – because they had made a vow to St Patrick, according to Irish accounts. Their victory feast was gruesome; in the words of Professor Shetelig:

> After the battle, messengers from Maelsechlainn, the High King of Ireland, came to the Danes. They found the army encamped on the very battlefield, engaged in cooking their meat. The cauldrons were placed on top of heaps of fallen Norwegians, with spits stuck in among the bodies, and the fires burning them so that their bellies burst, revealing the welter of meat and pork eaten the night before. The messengers reproached them for such conduct, but they answered that their enemies would have wished to do the same to them. The Danes, in accordance with their promise, gave a big chest of gold and silver to St Patrick, 'for,' says the chronicle, 'the Danes had at least a kind of piety; they were for piety's sake capable of ceasing for a while from their eating and drinking.'

However, the Norwegians rallied, and three years later regained control of Ireland, so that no Danish colony was ever established there.

The greatest Viking enterprise in the early tenth century was the colonization of Normandy, but unfortunately French sources are very scanty from 882 to about 920 – precisely the decades when this colony was being established. It is practically certain that, when in 911 Charles the Simple ceded Normandy to Rollo in exchange for a promise that he would defend France against other Vikings, he was only ratifying an existing state of affairs, and that Rollo had been securely ensconced in Normandy for some while. Like the Danelaw, Normandy is full of Scandinavian place-names; these show that the settlers were mostly Danes (even if, as Norse sources state, Rollo himself was Norwegian), and that some of them apparently had previously been living in the Danelaw.

The middle decades of the tenth century saw no further Viking expansion into Europe. In France, Rollo and his successors kept would-be raiders at bay; in England, the Wessex kings made war against the Danelaw and reasserted English overlordship over these territories, which they temporarily achieved in 927. Further power struggles broke out in the next two decades, during which Northumbria was sometimes ruled by men who acknowledged the English kings as overlord, and sometimes by more independent kings. On the whole, the Danes seem to have been fairly quick to give allegiance to English kings, probably because they wanted their help against their rivals, the Norwegians of Ireland and north-west England, with whom they were struggling for the control of York; in any case, English overlordship was purely political, and did nothing to interfere with the steady growth of the Danelaw settlements. The whole period was one of quiet consolidation in the various Scandinavian colonies from Iceland to Normandy, and the few raids which occurred (as for instance by Norwegians roving round Spain and the Mediterranean in the 960s) were the daring enterprises of individuals, not part of a mass movement.

After 50 years of peace, England was attacked again in the 980s. There followed two decades of intensive raids, characterized by a technique which was new to England, though it had been used in France 100 years before – the payment of 'Danegelds' to buy local peace from the attackers. The nature of the raiding bands had also changed: Swedes (hitherto only interested in the Baltic and Russian areas) joined with Norwegians and Danes, and mixed forces from all three nations sailed round the English coasts, showing no interest in settlement, but only in exacting more and yet more silver. One fleet of 94 ships, led by the future kings Olaf Tryggvason of Norway and Svein Forkbeard of Denmark, tried to attack London in 994, and subsequently were paid 16,000 pounds of silver as their price for ceasing to ravage south-east England.

In 1002 Ethelred the Unready, driven to desperation by raids and rumours of conspiracy, ordered a massacre 'of all the Danes in England' (i.e. in the south, not in the Danelaw), even those who were settlers or hired soldiers in his own service. Among those slaughtered were the sister and brother-in-law of Svein, now King of Denmark. The inevitable result was that Svein attacked England in greater force than ever, and was only persuaded to withdraw after payment of 36,000 pounds of silver. In 1009 there arrived a fresh fleet of Norwegians and Danes, led by Thorkel the Tall, one of the chieftains of the famous Jomsvikings, a band of professional warriors with their headquarters in the Baltic. For three years he ravaged England, but eventually he accepted a Danegeld of 48,000 pounds, paid off most of his men, and himself remained with 45 of his ships as mercenaries in the service of Ethelred.

In July 1013 Svein returned, and set about the wholesale conquest of England; the whole Danelaw accepted him at once, and despite some opposition by Thorkel's men, by Christmas Svein was king of all England and Ethelred was fleeing to Normandy. Svein, however, died the next February, and Ethelred returned; there followed a two-year struggle in which Svein's son Cnut (Canute the Great), with armies drawn from three Scandinavian countries, tried to win England for himself. After the deaths of Ethelred and of Edmund Ironside in 1016, there was no one to oppose him, and Cnut, at the age of 20, became sole king of England.

The period of full Danish rule in England (1017–42) must certainly have meant an increase in Scandinavian influence all over the country, with Danes of high rank being granted estates in various regions, not merely in the Danelaw. It may also be assumed that a few of the rank and file of Cnut's men joined the settlers; but by far the greater number went home in 1018, when Cnut disbanded his fleets and armies, distributing among them the huge sum of 82,500 pounds of silver, the last and greatest Danegeld levied in England.

The men of Svein's and Cnut's armies were well-organized mercenaries seeking wealth, not primarily from haphazard looting, but from the systematic extortion of Danegelds. Their silver returned with them to Scandinavia, where many thousands of English coins of this period have been found. Thanks to the Swedish custom of raising memorial stones, we even know the names of several Swedes who 'took Danegeld' in England and proudly had the fact inscribed on their memorials, sometimes with the name of the leader they had fought under. Most interesting of these is the stone of Ulf of Borresta, who took a share in the pay-out of three Danegelds, twice under leaders whose names are famous in history. His stone reads:

Ulf had taken three gelds in England. The first was that which Tosti paid. Then Thorkel [the Tall] paid. Then Cnut paid.

The last decades of the tenth century, which saw these large-scale military enterprises and political conflicts, also saw the final stages in the westward migrations of Norse farming settlers – the colonization of Greenland, and the attempt to settle some part of America. The story of these undertakings is told in two sagas, *The Saga of the Greenlanders* (believed to date from before 1200), and *The Saga of Eirik the Red* (mid-thirteenth century); there are also allusions to the discoveries in other medieval works, including a reference to 'Vinland', i.e. America, as early as 1075 in the writings of Adam of Bremen. In addition to literary sources, the numerous remains of Norse buildings in Greenland cast much light on the settlement there, and now at last there is sound archaeological evidence that Norsemen reached the American continent.

The settlement of Greenland began in 982, when an Icelander named Eirik the Red was banished for three years for manslaying, and decided to

Memorial stone to Ulf of Borresta, Sweden.

spend the time exploring an unknown land to the west, accidentally discovered several decades previously but never properly surveyed. For three years he explored the south and west coasts, living by hunting and fishing, and apparently suffering no casualties among his crew; on his return home, 'he called the land he had discovered "Greenland", for he said that men would be far more tempted to go there if it had an attractive name'. There were indeed reasons why the Icelanders should feel tempted. Their farming methods required ample grassland, but by this time all the best areas had been taken, leaving no further room for late comers; moreover, only 10 years before, Iceland had suffered a grim famine, in which

> men ate ravens and foxes, and many loathsome things were eaten which should not be eaten, and some men had the old and helpless killed and thrown over the cliffs. Many starved to death, while others took to stealing, and were condemned and put to death for it. Even outlaws killed each other, for . . . it was made law that anyone who killed three outlaws should go free.

Eirik found many men willing to follow him. In the summer of 986 he sailed for Greenland, accompanied by 25 shiploads of settlers and their livestock, though in fact only 14 reached their destination, the rest being wrecked or driven back. But in the next few years others followed, and formed two main settlement areas, of which one eventually held 190 farms and the other 90. It had been reckoned that at the height of their prosperity there must have been some 3,000 Norsemen in the Greenland colony.

Reconstruction of Thjodhild's church, Greenland.

Their stone and turf dwellings survive in large numbers; so too do the

churches built after their conversion. The oldest of these is a tiny chapel raised in about 1001 by Thjodhild, the wife of Eirik the Red, much against her husband's wishes; it was excavated in 1962. Internally, it measures only about 16 by 8 feet; most of the walls were of turf, but that at the west end must have been of wood, for it has entirely disappeared. *Eirik's Saga* tells how Thjodhild had her church built 'not too near the farm', so as not to infuriate her heathen husband; excavation confirms this, and shows that she even chose a site where the natural lie of the land would completely hide it from the farmstead. There were about 150 skeletons buried round it (men on the south side, women on the north); they presumably include Thjodhild herself and her famous son Leif the Lucky.

Greenland farming was based on rearing cattle, sheep and goats, just as in Iceland; there was enough grass to support considerable herds, judging by the size of the cattle-byres – those of an average farm would hold 10 to 20 cows, and those of Brattahlid (Eirik's own farm) about 40. Curiously enough, drought seems to have been a problem; there are remains of long irrigation channels and dykes crossing the meadows at Brattahlid, and similar systems elsewhere. A Norwegian text of about 1225 gives details about diet that are exactly confirmed by what was found in the middens of Brattahlid:

> It is said that in Greenland there are good pastures, and that there are large and fine farms. . . . The farmers there raise many cattle and sheep, and make much butter and much cheese; they live mainly on these foods and on beef, and they also eat meat and game of many kinds, such as the flesh of caribou, whale, seals or bears.

From the same source we learn that the Greenlanders tried to grow grain, with very little success, and that they systematically explored the country, climbing the highest mountains 'to look about and learn whether any land could be found that was free from ice and habitable'. Nor were they cut off from their kinsmen overseas; ships plied regularly to Norway and Iceland, bearing such valuable exports as walrus ivory, whalebone, ropes of walrus and seal hides, soapstone, bearskins and other furs, and even narwhal tusks (for sale as unicorn horns); living polar bears and falcons were also highly prized. The main imports must have been grain (for beer and bread), and iron tools, for though Greenland did yield some rather inferior bog-iron, there was extremely little suitable fuel for working it. It may be added that many climatologists believe that up to about 1100 the climate was warmer in those regions than it is today; the seas must have been freer of ice, and the conditions more favourable for cattle-raising.

The colony proved tenacious. Despite many difficulties and deteriorating circumstances, and despite growing conflict with the Eskimos, there were still Norsemen there in 1406–10, busily celebrating a wedding, burning a suspected wizard at the stake, and giving hospitality to a party of Icelanders storm-bound on their shores. But these Icelanders were the last ever to bring reliable news from Greenland; how exactly the colony died out is unknown, but by the sixteenth century Eskimos were once more the sole inhabitants.

The discovery of America had followed hard upon that of Greenland, of which it was the natural and almost inevitable consequence. Paradoxically, the fact that two sagas tell the story has increased the difficulties of historians, for they disagree on several particulars; much ink has been spilt arguing over their respective merits, and trying to extract precise geographical information from them. Among other discrepancies, they give the credit of first discovery to different men. *The Saga of the Greenlanders* speaks of a certain Bjarni who, late in 986, set out to follow the fleet of colonizers who had sailed from Iceland for Greenland, but drifted far to the south-west in a fog; three times he sighted a strange coast, but it never corresponded to what he had heard about Greenland, so he sailed doggedly north-east without landing, till at last he found his way to Greenland itself. Only in about 990 did Leif the Lucky, a son of Eirik the Red, decide to take a closer look at these unknown lands, using Bjarni's information to retrace his course in the opposite direction. *Eirik's Saga*, on the contrary, ignores Bjarni altogether and ascribes the glory to Leif alone, dating his journey to about 1003. Modern scholars are inclined to consider *The Saga of the Greenlanders* the more reliable and older of the two accounts; it is therefore not strictly true to call Leif the 'discoverer' of America, though he can fairly be called the first European to land upon the continent and explore it.

It is beyond the scope of this chapter to analyse the saga accounts, which have been vigorously debated. There were several expeditions covering hundreds of miles of coast, from the rocky shores of 'Helluland' (Baffin Island?), past the forests of 'Markland' (Labrador?), to warmer regions where grapes grew wild and inspired the explorers to coin the name 'Vinland', 'Wine Land'. The purpose was of course to found permanent settlements, and one party stayed about two years; but, according to both sagas, every attempt was eventually foiled by the hostility of the native 'Skrælings', Red Indians and/or Eskimos. Yet, though colonization apparently proved impossible, various scraps of information strongly suggest that Greenlanders long continued to visit these regions, to fetch better timber than the driftwood on their own beaches.

In 1965 came the publication of the 'Vinland Map' – a widely-publicized document which, it was claimed, had been made in the Upper Rhineland in about 1440. It shows the whole of the Old World as then known, together with many islands dotted about the Western Ocean, including a remarkably accurate Greenland and, to the south-west of this, a huge island labelled 'Island of Vinland, found by Bjarni and Leif in company'. The editors believed that the representation of Greenland must be copied from some lost Icelandic map of the thirteenth or early fourteenth century, which in turn was based on the practical knowledge of the Greenlanders themselves; the drawing of Vinland, on the other hand, they thought was not based on experience, but was a medieval reconstruction from the data in the sagas (which existed in manuscripts well before the map, if genuine, was made).

The map bears a few Latin captions, of which the most important is that in the top left corner; this, after repeating the claim that 'the companions Bjarni and Leif Eiriksson' discovered Vinland together, goes on:

> Eirik, legate of the Apostolic See and bishop of Greenland and the neighbouring regions, arrived in this truly vast and very rich land, in the name of Almighty God, in the last year of our most blessed father Pascal [i.e. Pope Pascal II, died 1118], remained a long time in both summer and winter, and later returned northeastwards towards Greenland, and then went on his way in most humble obedience to the will of his superiors.

However, the very accuracy of the delineation of Greenland raised doubts of the map's authenticity among some geographers, for there was no previous evidence that medieval Icelanders made maps, or that the Greenland colonists had circumnavigated their huge land. Other scholars felt equally suspicious of the Latin captions which, while neatly reconciling the contradiction between the two sagas as to the identity of the 'discoverer', added so little fresh information about the actual voyages of discovery. The sensational claim that the Apostolic Legate had spent a whole year on American soil, presumably ministering to the needs of settlers there, was supported by no other documentary evidence. Eventually, in response to growing scepticism, new and more refined scientific tests were allowed to be carried out on the map itself; as a result, it was announced in 1974 that the ink used in drawing it had been proved to contain a chemical pigment (titanium iodide) which had only been used in inks since 1920. The 'Vinland Map' must therefore rank as a forgery – by far the cleverest hoax yet attempted in the field of Norse studies, and one which achieved great initial success. It must be stressed, however, that this forgery in no way undermines the value of the saga accounts themselves; it merely deprives them of what at first had seemed interesting supplementary support.

It has long been hoped that archaeology would confirm and supplement the written sources by producing material proof of Norse activity on the American continent, either by finds of American objects in the Greenland settlements, or, preferably, of Norse artefacts in America. There have been two important discoveries of the first kind: several larch-wood coffins were found at Herjolfsnes in south Greenland, larch being common in Newfoundland and Labrador, but unknown in Scandinavia; and an arrowhead of Labrador quartzite, made in Red Indian fashion, was found in the Norse churchyard at Sandnes in western Greenland. The larch could be explained away as driftwood, but the arrow-head can surely only have been brought by some Norseman returning from an expedition in which he had encountered American Indians.

The search for Norse relics on the American continent has led to several fakes and false hopes, but reliable evidence seems at last to have appeared. In 1961 Dr Helge Ingstad and his wife began a series of excavations at L'Anse-aux-Meadows, on the northern tip of the Island of Newfoundland. They reported finding a group of dwellings, including one that seems to be a long-house with a central hearth, and others with heaps of fire-cracked stones or with a stone-lined ember-pit – all well-known features in Viking Age houses in Greenland, Iceland and elsewhere (Chapter 3). Near by, a small smithy yielded lumps of local bog-iron, 30 pounds of slag, scraps of worked iron, one piece of bronze, some charcoal, a stone anvil, a hearth, and a firepit. This is highly significant, for neither Eskimos nor Indians were capable of metal working, while at the same time the techniques seem too primitive for men of Columbus's time. Carbon-14 tests on the charcoal produced the highly satisfactory datings of 1060 (plus or minus 70 years) and 890 (plus or minus 90 years); tests on turf from the walls also yielded dates ranging from about 900 to the eleventh century. Another crucial find was reported late in 1964: a soapstone whorl of the very common type used by Norse women to weight their spindles. This is exactly the type of evidence which would most valuably supplement the saga accounts, as it would indicate the presence of true settlers, accompanied by their womenfolk and practising their usual crafts. In 1968 came a further report of a find of bronze jewellery dating from around 1000. The publication of Dr Ingstad's full report will surely prove a major development in the discussion of the Vinland Voyages, the furthest and most romantic enterprise of the land-hungry Norsemen.

Huntsman with hawk and hound, from a Swedish stone.

3
Life on the Land

There are such wide variations in climate and soil conditions between the various areas inhabited by Scandinavians of the Viking Age that it is impossible to do justice here to the full range of their techniques in agriculture and animal husbandry. Roughly speaking, it can be said that in wide regions of Denmark, south-eastern Sweden, and many south-western valleys of Norway, there was extensive cultivation of cereals, as well as cattle-breeding; the further north one goes, the greater is the part played by the livestock, though even in Iceland cereal crops could still be grown. There is a broadly corresponding difference in the pattern of habitation; in southern areas, especially in Denmark, farms are clustered together in true villages, presumably with a system of cultivated field-strips and common grazing lands similar to those in medieval England. But where cattle-rearing predominated, the first necessity was that each farm should have its own ample grasslands, and so each would be set as far from its neighbour as the pressure of population allowed. This tendency reached its fullest development in Iceland, where villages and the communal sharing of agricultural tasks were utterly unknown.

The northern regions and the western settlements also depended more on hunting wild animals and birds to improve their food supplies. The natural resources were indeed very rich: sea-birds were shot or snared, and their eggs collected; there were herring and cod in the seas, trout and salmon in the rivers; whales were harpooned, or rounded up and driven ashore to die, as was done in the Faroes until very recent times; seals were speared or netted; bears, wild boars, elk, red deer and reindeer could all be hunted in the mountains of Scandinavia. In winter, huntsmen went on skis; which is why the same deities, Ull and Skadi, were patrons of skiing, archery and hunting.

Spearing fish: detail from a Gotland stone.

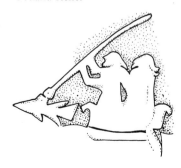

Falconry was practised, though even at this period it seems to have been an aristocrat's pursuit. Fish were taken with baited lines, nets, fish-spears or traps; it is even possible that fly-fishing was known, for in some Old Icelandic expressions 'fly' is used metaphorically for 'lure' or 'bait'. Sometimes there were deliberate attempts to improve natural resources; for instance, there are trout in certain high mountain lakes of Norway where they can only have been introduced by human agency, and an eleventh-century rune-stone records that the man for whom it was raised 'brought the fish' to one such little lake.

It must be remembered that all this hunting and trapping played a much wider part in the economy than merely satisfying a local wish for a varied diet. The furs, bearskins and reindeer hides of northern Scandinavia were valuable articles for export; so too were walrus hides and sealskins, walrus ivory, whale-oil, whalebone, feathers, live falcons, and perhaps dried fish. The various uses of the land's resources all affected one another and contributed to the general economy, as can be seen, for instance, in the exploitation of the Norwegian mountain regions. Each summer these were visited by three groups of seasonal workers: the fur-trappers, the iron workers coming to smelt ore from the mountain bogs (and incidentally to make charcoal for their needs), and the herdsmen driving cattle and sheep to pasture on the upland grass and scrub. The first two indirectly helped the third, for the trapping of wild beasts made the uplands safer for the flocks, and the felling of wood for charcoal cleared new land for grazing; at the same time, skins, furs and iron supplied needs in the valley farms and also were traded with the coastal dwellers and exported to the south.

Differences in climate naturally also affected the construction of houses and other farm buildings. Where timber was plentiful and winters not too severe, houses were built of wood by any of several methods: vertical planking set edge-to-edge ('stave-building'), horizontal planking set between vertical posts ('bul-building'), wattle-and-daub, or horizontal logs. Excavations in Dublin have uncovered many buildings walled with wattles set between posts and a three-roomed stave-built house on wooden foundations. But there also existed an old tradition of building with thick walls of earth, stones, and turf, and a roof of turf; for this, wood was only needed for roof supports and for internal features such as partitions and panelling, while the whole structure was warmer than a timbered house. This method therefore spread to the wet, cold, and treeless Atlantic colonies.

In the Orkneys, Shetlands and the Faroes men used local stone, sometimes in pure drystone walling, but more often surrounding a core of earth or alternating with layers of turf. Methods often reflect local conditions; for instance, in the Shetlands, the first Norse house built on the Jarlshof site used turf in its north wall only, to obtain extra warmth where it was needed most. In Iceland, where there is hardly any stone fit for building, men developed a skilful technique of building in pure turf. Turf was also much used in Greenland, but for the sake of warmth, not because suitable stone was lacking. Large timbers needed for internal structures had to be imported or obtained from driftwood.

Materials varied, but the shape of a farmhouse (as distinct from a square town house) was basically similar in all Scandinavian lands. The earliest form was the one-roomed long-house, which might be anything from 40 to 100 feet in length. Its two longer walls curved inwards quite markedly towards the gable ends, a traditional feature alleged to date from primitive times when houses were roofed with an upturned boat; several strong posts were arranged in two rows down the middle of the building to take the weight of the roof; down each side of the room ran a broad, low, flattened bank of earth, its edge held up by boards or slabs of stone, to form a smooth raised floor; the central strip was left as a rough lower floor, in which was set at least one long stone-lined hearth, and often a cooking-pit as well.

This type of dwelling already had a long history behind it by the time of the Vikings; in earlier centuries it had housed animals as well as men, but by this period it seems that cattle had everywhere been banished into separate byres, either built end-to-end with the dwelling house (as at Unst, and in the second house at Jarlshof), or beside it (as at Kvivik, where the byre and barn were combined into one building alongside the house), or standing some way off. Nevertheless, the one-roomed long-house was still the scene of all indoor activities; *Grettir's Saga* calls such buildings 'fire-halls', and describes them as they existed in the tenth century in Iceland:

> It was the custom in those times that there should be large fire-halls on the farmsteads. Men would sit there by the long fires in the evenings. It was there that tables were set in front of people [for their meal], and afterwards they would sleep up beside the fires. Also the women would work at their wool there during the day.

But the one-roomed long-house was often divided by wooden partitions which cut off some small section at one end or both, to serve as storerooms or as sleeping-quarters more private than the communal hall. From this there arose a later form of long-house divided into two or three rooms set end-to-end; at about the same time the walls lost their earlier characteristic curve. The first step was to separate the kitchen from the combined living- and sleeping-room, and the next to develop a sort of entrance-hall, whose purpose is not precisely known; next, the daytime living-room might be separated from the sleeping-quarters. Finally, it became the custom to build small extra rooms on to the back of the house for storage; this multi-roomed long-house continued to be built beyond the Viking Age, but was eventually replaced in Iceland and Greenland by another type in which rooms were grouped round a central passage.

Three variations on the long-house pattern can be seen among farmsteads excavated in the Icelandic valley of Thjorsardal. The early stage is represented by the house at Isleifsstadir, which dates from the Settlement Period; it has a very large main room, from which only two small areas are partitioned off at one end.

Probably equally old, but further developed, is Skalakot. One of its two doorways leads into an entrance-hall, from which a small area has been partitioned off against the gable wall. The middle of the building is a long main room, with its raised earthen side-floors divided up by rows of stones, and with a long central hearth. At the far end of the building, beyond the second, well-paved, doorway, is a deep cooking-pit; this end therefore was clearly the kitchen area, and may well have been partitioned off as a separate room. The three small rooms at the back of the house do not appear to be as old as the rest of it, and must have been added to suit later fashions; two were

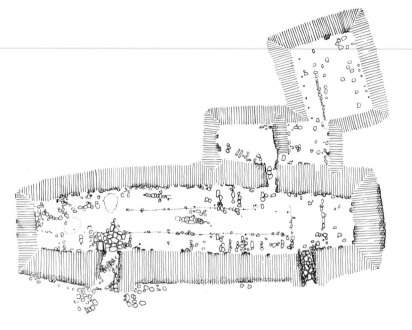

Excavation plan of the
longhouse at Skalakot.

storerooms, but the third had several small hearths, and so may have
replaced the older kitchen.

The full development can be seen at Stöng. Here again there is an
entrance-hall, with one biggish corner partitioned off. Then comes a fine
main room, with broad raised side-floors, probably boarded over, a central
hearth, and stone slabs as foundations for the roof-posts. The walls had been
covered with wooden panelling; this was a frequent feature in such houses,
and we learn from sagas that panelling, roof-posts and doorposts might all
be decoratively carved. There is a third, smaller, room; this too has panelling
and raised side-floors, though the latter are so narrow that they can only
have been meant for seats, not sleeping-places; it has three hearths, and in
one corner stood a loom. Evidently in this house people still ate and slept in
the big central room, but in the daytime the women went to a separate room
for their weaving, and perhaps they also cooked there. Two small
storerooms opened off the back; the first held three large storage vats for
dairy produce (one still showing traces of curds when excavated). The floor
of the other was crossed by two deep stone gulleys, and the excavator, Aage
Roussel, suggests that these were packed with ice, and meat kept in cold
storage over them; an alternative suggestion is that the room was a lavatory
with seats for several people over the gulleys.

But there is far more to a farm than just a dwelling-house. One of the best
sites so far uncovered for the study of a whole complex of buildings is
Jarlshof in the Shetlands, where one can watch the growth of a farm over
several hundred years – the addition of new houses as the descendants of the
first settlers multiplied, the building and re-building of byres, stables, barns

and other outhouses, even the use and disuse of boundary walls, muck-heaps, and flagged bases for haystacks.

The illustration below shows Jarlshof as it was in the middle of the ninth century. *A* is the original long-house built by the first settlers some 40 or 50 years before; it consists simply of a smallish kitchen and a large main room, and has a fine stone pavement outside its northern wall. *B* is a second long-house recently built for a younger branch of the family; it is divided

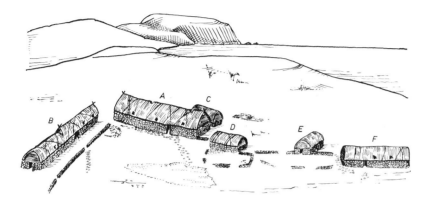

Reconstruction of the Jarlshof settlement *c*.850.

into two sections with no internal communication between them, the southern section being the not very spacious living-quarters, and the northern section a cowhouse built so that its entrance faces down the slope. The small outhouse *C* has several internal partitions, and was probably a privy. *D* is a stable, with cobbled flooring. *E* is a smithy, where a stone anvil, an open hearth, and lumps of iron slag were found. *F* is either a barn or byre. Of the various outhouses, both *C* and *D* are new, contemporary with *B*; whereas *E* and *F* go back to the first phase of the settlement. In that earliest phase there had been two other outhouses, one apparently for native Picts kept as slaves by the newly arrived Vikings, but both are now in ruins and buried under piles of refuse. Of the various walls surrounding the courtyards, some are recent, but others were built by the Picts who lived on this site before the Vikings came.

Sites such as Jarlshof and the Greenland settlements place our knowledge of Norse farmsteads on a sound archaeological basis, but it is the literature of Iceland that adds colour to the picture by its detailed accounts of life in a farming community. The rest of this chapter, therefore, will offer a general description of the yearly and daily round of activities on an Icelandic farmstead.

Only about 13 per cent of Iceland can be inhabited by men whose economy is based on cattle and sheep. The settlers took possession of every grassy region, whether along the coastal strip or up the valleys that pierce deep into the country; even the tiniest little upland dale had its occupier. The leaders in the first wave took massive holdings, from which they allotted land to kinsmen and followers, and later to their grown sons, and even to their freedmen. In 930 a law was passed limiting the amount of land which newcomers might claim: a man should have only as much as he could walk round in one day, carrying fire with him; a woman, as much as she could walk round in one day, leading a two-year-old cow. Such a holding would still be considerable, to be measured in miles rather than acres; even when the population had increased and the estates had been many times subdivided, it was still characteristic of Icelandic farms that they lay far apart.

The favourite sites were high on the grassy slopes, near the foot of the mountains and facing lower land, and with a stream close at hand. Sometimes a conduit would be dug to bring water right up to the farm buildings; in Greenland, Eirik the Red went one better, for his house had a stream running in a stone-lined, stone-covered channel across the floor of the main room itself.

A farm consisted of many different buildings, some in a close cluster round the dwelling-house, some scattered over the meadows several hundred yards away. All had low, thick walls and roofs whose layers of turf had grown into a solid grassy mass, so that they looked like little hillocks. On such roofs children could play and dogs bask in the sun, and even full-grown men could safely walk on them; sometimes cattle or goats might clamber up to eat the turf and have to be chased away.

The inner cluster of buildings included the byre and stables, and a hay-barn which might be built right up against the byre. If there were sheep-sheds (which was not always the case, for in some parts of Iceland sheep could be left in the open all winter), they would be further off across the meadows; there were various special buildings for lambs and milch ewes. Pigsties and goat-sheds might also be needed. Also at some distance from the farmhouse would be more barns, for reserves of hay and grain. If the farm was on the coast, there would be a shed into which the farmer's boat was dragged on rollers for the winter, and a hut with open slatted walls in which raw fish was dried by the wind blowing through it.

The domestic buildings usually included a smithy, somewhat isolated because of the risk of fire, and a bath-house. The baths were steam-baths, like a modern Finnish *sauna*, and were taken in a special little building with a stone-flagged floor, and a drain to carry off the water, and either a stone oven or an open hearth over which piles of stones could be heated red-hot in a peat fire. Water would then be thrown over the hot stones to fill the room with steam. There was a sort of high platform or shelf round the walls, and those who wanted to swelter in the greatest heat would climb up on to it. The bathers would whip themselves with bundles of twigs, and often end with a cold douche or by rolling in the snow. Sometimes Icelanders also bathed in the hot pools of their volcanic springs; there is a famous pool, still well preserved, on the estate which once belonged to Snorri Shuluson, and it is known to have already been in use in his time.

There would of course be storehouses, the keys of which were kept by the mistress of the house. Those for perishable foods such as dairy produce,

bread or fresh meat would be near the main house, if not actually built on to
it; further off were those for dried and salted foods, or for tools, harness,
ropes, bales of cloth, and suchlike things. There are occasional mentions of
'earth-houses', underground chambers whose normal use would presumably be for food storage (though when they are spoken of it is usually as
hiding-places for fugitives).

In front of every farm lay the homefield, carefully tended and manured to
produce the finest hay, and fenced in by walls of turf or stone to keep all
animals out – except perhaps for the 'homefield boar', a single pig allowed in
to fatten on its rich grasses. Further off lay other meadows of good-quality
grass, walled in but not manured, and the ploughed fields for the grain
crops. There was no vegetable-plot; Icelanders ate hardly any greenstuffs,
only a few wild plants such as angelica and a species of leek, and certain
edible seaweeds.

Everyone took a share in the farm work. It may have been the case that in
the Scandinavian homelands wealthy landowners left manual labours to
slaves and servants; for instance, it seems to have been thought odd that the

Hot-water bathing pool at
Snorri's farmstead.

stepfather of Olaf the Saint worked in the fields among his men, and he was nicknamed Sigurd the Sow in consequence. In Iceland, however, the hard tasks of pioneering broke down this distinction, and sagas describe even the greatest chieftains as working on the land, though naturally not at the heaviest unskilled work.

The first settlers brought many slaves, mostly captives from Scotland, Ireland and the Isles; supplies could easily be renewed by purchase or by further raiding, and it is likely that slavery did not entirely die out in Iceland until the early twelfth century. Yet it seems always to have been quite common to free a slave in reward for good service, or to let him earn money to buy his liberty; such freed slaves were generally given a small plot of land on their former master's estate, where they could set themselves up as cottars, though often still partly dependent on the paid work he would give them. The clearest account of such arrangements does not relate to Iceland, but to a wealthy Norwegian chieftain early in the eleventh century:

> Erling always had 30 slaves at home on his farm, besides other servants. He would allot the day's work to his slaves, but after this would give them their time free, with permission to every man who so wished to work for himself in the evening and at night. He gave them ploughlands to sow corn for themselves, and let them use the crop for their own profit. He would assign a particular amount of work to each, to win himself freedom by doing it; and there were many who earned their freedom in this way in one year, or in the second year, and all who had any capacity for work could make themselves free within three years. With this money he bought other slaves. He taught some of his freed men how to work at herring fishing, and taught a useful craft to others, and some cleared fresh land for themselves, and built themselves farmhouses. In this way he set them all on the road to prosperity.

There were also many free men and women working as farm-hands, and receiving board and lodging for themselves and their dependents; in later times they also drew fixed legal wages, but it is not clear how far this system was in force in the Viking Age. They were hired by the year, some to do a specified task, such as looking after an allotted number of cattle or sheep, and others as general workers who would turn their hands to whatever was needed. Simple routine jobs of smithying or carpentry would be done by some member of the household, but for more elaborate work a specialized craftsman from elsewhere would be called in, and such a man would be paid an agreed sum for his work.

The farmer's year began when the snows melted and the cattle were brought from the byres to graze on the new grass. Icelandic months do not coincide with ours, and this particular season, which was reckoned the first month of the summer half-year, began in mid-April. It has two names, Cuckoo Month and Sowing Time, for this was also the season for ploughing and the sowing of the cereal crops. These were mainly barley, oats and bere (an older variety of barley); wheat could be grown in a few sheltered regions, but rye was impossible so far north. Iceland also had lyme-grass growing wild; the poorer people sometimes used its grain, and in Greenland, where other cereals were very hard to grow, it was deliberately cultivated. There were two types of plough, the ancient 'ard', which had no mould-board and was very light, and the far more developed 'wheel-plough', with mould-board, coulter, and wheels supporting the beam. They were usually drawn by oxen, one man guiding the plough and another walking ahead to encourage the oxen with a long stick, or to check them if the ploughshare wedged against a stone. After the ploughing, the seed would be sown and harrowed in.

Other tasks for early spring were peat-digging and wood-cutting to replenish stocks of fuel, and the repairing of the walls round the meadows and homefield, which had probably suffered from frost and snow. This was a lengthy but very necessary task, for as the grass grew higher it had to be kept safe from wandering animals if the vital hay crop was to be successful. At the same time too, the homefield would be manured with dung that had accumulated all winter in the byres and sheep-sheds; in later centuries, when Iceland's woods had vanished, dried dung was used for fuel, but this was not yet necessary in the Viking Age.

The month that ran from mid-May to mid-June was called either Egg Time or Lambs' Fold Time. The first does not refer to poultry keeping, but to the gathering of eggs from the wild seabirds that nest in millions round the coasts and on the little islands of the fjords. The lambs were weaned, the flocks were sheared, and towards mid-June would begin the great summer migration to the hills, in which almost all the cattle and sheep would be driven high into the upland pastures. Only a few beasts would be kept down at the main farm to supply the immediate needs for milk.

Up on the mountains each farm had its shieling, a small house where many of the household lived during the summer months. The milch cows and ewes would be kept together by the herdsmen, fairly near the shielings, but the other animals were left to roam freely. The women did the milking and made dairy products, a much-valued part of Scandinavian diet: fresh butter, and, more important, the long-lasting butter made from sour cream and strongly salted; soft cheese from sour fermenting milk; and *skyr*, a tasty form of cheesy curds. Full milk was rarely drunk, but the whey was, either plain or boiled or made into buttermilk. For all these purposes the milk of sheep and goats was as much used as that of cows. It seems that life in the shielings was the gayest and most pleasant part of the year's routine; from it the period of late June and early July took its names: Shieling Month, or Sun Month.

Since, meanwhile, there was less pressure of work down at the main farmstead, this was the best time of the year for long journeys. In every district a small local Assembly (or 'Thing') had been held towards the middle of May for the settling of minor lawsuits, but the General Assembly of Iceland, for which men must gather from all over the country, was timed to take place during this comparatively slack period. Every farmer of

substance had to attend, and usually he would be accompanied by his family and a good number of followers who would support him in his lawsuits; the whole party might be away from home for three weeks or more. Other journeys were also undertaken round midsummer; at this season merchant ships arrived from Norway and men would gather at the coast to trade with them. Dairy products would also be sent down to the coasts on packhorses, to be bartered for the dried fish and salt of the seaside farmers.

In the second half of July began the Haymaking Month; in fact, haymaking continued all during August, and into part of September too. On its success depended the fodder for the coming winter, so every available man and woman was pressed into service. Not only were the homefield and the walled meadows mown, but as much as possible of the open country too. All this grass was scythed and raked into swathes, tossed and turned at intervals to dry it, and at last dragged to the farm on carts and sledges; as much as possible was stored in barns, and the rest built into haystacks, which were protected against the weather by turf or thatching.

The haymaking overlapped with the harvesting of the cereal crops, from which late August and early September took their name, Corn Cutting Month. Then followed Autumn Month, which lasted to mid-October, and was reckoned the last month of the summer half-year. In the course of it the cattle, sheep and goats would be rounded up from the mountain pastures, where they might have strayed for many miles and joined other men's herds. All would have to be found, sorted out according to their earmarks, and

brought down into the valley. There the farmer, bearing in mind how much hay he had got in, would reckon how many beasts he could hope to keep alive over the winter; the remainder would be slaughtered, and their meat dried or salted.

The beginning of winter was a good time for weddings and other feasts, there being plenty of fresh meat and ale; in heathen times it was the season for one of the main festivals of the year. However, there was still much work to be done. As in spring, the homefield walls had to be put in good repair, this time in order to keep the haystacks safe from the remaining livestock, which would still graze out of doors near the farms for as long as the weather allowed. On the other hand, walls round the cornfields were breached, so that the cattle could get at the stubble. Byres, stables and other buildings had to be put in order, and good supplies of fuel laid in in a final burst of peat-cutting.

The six winter months were a time for indoor work. Tools were repaired, the dressed hides and sheepskins from the autumn slaughtering were worked up into clothing, shoes, bed-coverings, harness and other useful articles; there was carpentry and boat-repairing to be done, and the carving of innumerable small objects in wood, bone or horn.

Meanwhile the livestock were cared for by shepherds and herdsmen; in some parts of Iceland sheep and goats had to be kept in shelters overnight, though they would be driven out in the daytime to feed on whatever they could find amid the snow; in other areas it was possible to keep them out

Reconstructed section of the Oseberg Tapestry, showing wagons, riders, and men and women on foot, interspersed with birds and decorative patterns.

night and day, even in the depth of winter. But cows could never stand such a system; they were kept in their byres all the time, and hay was brought to them there. In Greenland the settlers did all they could to keep the byres warm; some had walls five feet thick and a great mound of turf piled over them, with the entrance by a long, narrow, twisting passage to exclude the cold air; others were built in the middle of a tight-packed circle of buildings, so that the hardier sheep and goats in the outer ones would give warmth to the cattle in the centre. Conditions in Iceland were less severe, yet even so there must have been many losses among the livestock, and the surviving beasts must have been weak with hunger by the time spring came round again and the farmer's year began once more.

To some extent women too followed a seasonal routine, doing dairywork at the shielings and helping with haymaking and the harvest, but they also had a task that went on all the year round: the making of woollen cloth. This was not simply for their household needs, but for export to Norway or to England; cloth and sheepskins were almost the only goods Iceland could export at this period (her fish trade did not start till late in the Middle Ages), whereas there were many goods she needed from abroad. The survival of a farming household depended largely on the cattle, but its prosperity (and that of the Icelandic community as a whole) depended on the sheep.

When the wool had been carded out and cleaned of its grease, it was spun on a distaff and spindle. The distaff was held in the crook of the left arm, while the spindle, weighted at one end by a disk of stone (the 'spindle-whorl'), was set spinning by the right hand and sank slowly to the floor, drawing the wool out to a thread. This thread would be wound up, and the process repeated until a large ball of yarn had been produced. One great advantage of the method was that it could be practised while standing or walking; Norse women seem to have carried their spinning about with them everywhere, and one of the most characteristic finds in excavating a Viking Age house is a scattering of lost or discarded spindle-whorls.

Weaving was done on an upright loom propped against a wall, working from the top downwards. There were two sets of warp threads, held taut by stones hanging from them; horizontal rods controlled their relative positions as the woof was slipped through and beaten upwards with a wooden or whalebone 'sword'. The material was woven to a standard width, probably of two ells, and quality too was fairly standardized; lengths of the *vaðmál* (the undyed twill which was the staple product of Icelandic weaving) were used as an alternative unit to silver in reckoning prices, fines and other payments.

Other more valuable types of cloth were woven of dyed wool, often in stripes or patterns. The most usual dye was the red obtained from madder, which grows freely in Iceland; one could also get reddish-browns and violets from certain lichens, and black from bog-mud impregnated with iron. On one of the farms excavated in Thjorsardal red and green tufa-stone had been ground to powder in the smithy, showing that mineral dyes were known.

The most decorative patterned weaving was generally done on small looms which produced narrow bands of cloth. Still narrower strips, suitable

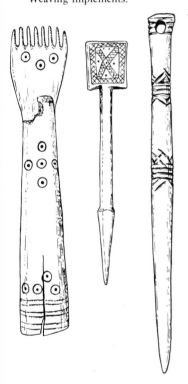

Weaving implements.

for trimming the edges of garments or for use as hair-bands, were made by the method known as 'tablet-weaving', which is still widely used all over Scandinavia; for this, the warp threads are passed through holes in the four corners of small square boards or bone plaques, and the patterns are produced by altering the relative positions of these. A loom of this type, with 52 tablets set ready for use, was found in the ship-burial at Oseberg. Many fine examples of tablet-weaving have been recovered from the Swedish graves at Birka, preserved by the silver and gold threads woven into them, and other fragments are known from Norway. The sagas frequently mention such decorative edging and ribbons; sometimes they imply that they were brought from abroad, not woven at home in Iceland, but there is no need to suppose that this was always the case.

Various types of needlework were also practised. There was embroidery with wool, with imported silk, and also with silver threads; it has been suggested that the latter were pricked directly into the material without the use of a needle, and pulled through with the little tweezers that are often found beside the scissors and needlecase in Norse women's graves. There

Tablet-weaving, from Birka.

Reconstruction of a loom.

was a simple kind of lace-making done by intertwining threads with bone needles. A widely practised skill, still used in Norway, was the making of ornamental snoods, borders and fringes by *sprang*, a kind of semi-knitting done on wooden needles and finished off by knotting.

Just as the Viking man was often buried with tools and weapons, so the women's graves, especially in Norway, contained equipment for textile work – distaffs and spindles, small looms, weaving 'swords', wool-combs, flax-heckles, scissors of many sizes, tweezers, needle-cases, and large bone needles. There are also flattened balls of glass whose bases often show signs of burning; these are thought to be smoothers for ironing seams and pleats on linen clothing. More puzzling are certain large whalebone plaques, slightly tapered, and often decorated at the wide end with animal heads. Possibly they were mangling boards, for rather similar wooden objects were so used in Holland and Scandinavia until recent times; after washing, the wet clothes would be wrapped round a wooden roller and rolled up and down the board, the latter being held by an animal-headed handle at the broad end. It is also possible that they were ironing boards, used in conjunction with the glass smoothers.

Sagas naturally often allude to clothes worn by persons living in the Viking Age, but it can be difficult to visualize the appearance of the objects of which they speak, or to be sure that they have not attributed a fashion of their own times to an earlier age. In describing clothes it is therefore best not to start from written sources but from archaeological evidence, especially the ornaments and other metal objects found in graves.

This evidence is clearest in the case of women, and is remarkably consistent over the whole area and period; changes of fashion there surely must have been, but they did not affect the basic costume. Viking women always wore a large pair of oval brooches, usually about four or five inches long, which archaeologists call 'tortoise brooches'; they were worn on the breast, almost at the collar-bones, and were linked by festoons of silver chains or beads. From the right-hand brooch hung other chains bearing a rather unwieldy assortment of objects – keys, knife, comb, scissors, needles, and perhaps a purse. In addition there was a third brooch worn on the middle of the chest, and this might be any of several shapes, long or square, three-lobed or round. The remaining jewels varied according to the owner's taste; finger-rings, arm-rings, pendants and necklaces of multi-coloured glass beads were all quite common.

The tortoise brooches of the Birka graves yielded a great deal of information about clothes and textiles, for their oxidation had preserved the material in contact with them and to which they had been pinned. It was thus discovered that these Swedish women wore a linen shift next to the skin, sometimes finely pleated; it may have had sleeves, but this cannot be proved. Over this came a twofold garment hanging from two loops held by the tortoise brooches, one set of loops being longer because it had to pass over the shoulders. A comparison with the folk-costume of later ages suggests that this double garment was two separate lengths of cloth wrapped

A Shetland longhouse, resembling a Viking house in its materials and general appearance.

Small Swedish figurines, probably representing Valkyries or female guardian spirits, and used as amulets.

round the body under the armpits, one from left to right and the other from right to left. Sometimes it was of wool, sometimes of linen, and the outer length was always of better quality than the inner. Over the whole thing came a shawl or cloak of fine wool, and it was the function of the third brooch to hold this in place. No trace of a belt-buckle has ever been found in a Viking woman's grave; either dresses hung loose, or they were held in by apron-strings or a knotted girdle.

The indications from these grave finds fit well with the dress of female figures on the Gotland stones (an especially clear one is the horn-bearing woman in the top panel of the stone shown on p. 181), on the Oseberg Tapestry, and some little silver figures of the ninth and tenth centuries. There is of course a strong likelihood that these represent supernatural women – Valkyries, goddesses, guardian spirits and the like – and that their attire is therefore ancient and traditional. However, as Scandinavian women seem to have been so conservative in their adornments, it is probably safe to assume that their dresses also changed little over the centuries.

These representations all agree in showing a robe that falls straight in front, often with some bands of ornament, and usually short enough to show the feet; at the back the robe is longer, trailing, and pleated; a shawl or cloak is drawn over the shoulders. As the figures are in profile, the jewellery does not show – unless the curious lumps on the shoulder and chest of one figurine shown on p. 54 indicate a brooch and string of beads. The hair is pulled back into a knot at the nape of the neck, from which it hangs loose down the back, possibly mingled with ribbons, but certainly not in a plait. Another figurine in this group has hair bound in a clubbed style; this woman is also unusual in being without a shawl and having a dress that seems pleated all

Implements for sewing, ironing, cooking and food-storage.

over. Even more unusual is the woman on a silver ornament shown below. She is seen from in front, seated, and one can clearly see four rows of beads across her chest, though if she is wearing tortoise brooches they are hidden by her flowing cloak; the curious object across the base of her neck is a very large type of brooch popular in Gotland a little before the Viking Age, specimens of which are often at least nine inches long.

The clothing shown looks rather light, and would certainly be supplemented by heavy cloaks and furs for winter. From the sagas we learn that women wore knee-length cloth leggings and some form of socks, and from the Oseberg burial we have several pairs of soft shoes of tanned leather.

Men's clothing showed far more variation than that of women, and a stronger taste for luxurious trimmings. It was from men's graves at Birka that the excavators recovered so many strips of cloth worked in gay patterns with silk or metal threads; some of these were evidently headbands and the brims of caps, while others were edgings, ribbons and appliqué work for the body-garments. Unfortunately the kind of brooch worn by men, the penannular type, cannot cover as much cloth as a tortoise brooch, and therefore these have not preserved the wool fabric they were pinned to. These graves do, however, show what objects men usually carried: knives, combs and buckled belts; pouches with metal frames and button fastenings; arm-rings and finger-rings; pendants, figurines, bells, or big single beads, worn hanging round the neck. Needless to say, men also carried weapons; these will be described in Chapter 6.

More can be learnt about men's clothing from the Gotland stones and the Oseberg Tapestry, supplemented by information from the sagas. Their upper garment was a tunic, closely fitting as far as the hips, then flaring slightly to its hem, which might come anywhere from mid-thigh to just below the knee. It had sleeves, so tight-fitting that they do not show up on the silhouettes of the stone-carved figures; it could be worn with or without a belt. The cut of the breeches varied greatly; some fell straight to the ankle like modern untapered trousers; some were very full and gathered in below the knee or at mid-calf, seeming almost as stiffly spread as Elizabethan hose; some, as we know from literary sources, clung very tightly to the leg, and it is probable that apparently bare-legged figures are in fact wearing these. According to the sagas, men also sometimes wore as under-garments linen pants and a short-sleeved shirt of linen or fine wool.

Cloaks were much worn. One Icelandic type was a square of sheepskins, or of cloth so shaggy that it looked like a fleece; King Harald Greycloak of Norway started a fashion for them at his court, as a favour to an Icelander who could find no buyers for a cargo of them, and thereby got his nickname. More stately are the very ample mantles worn by many figures on the Gotland stones, which show as pointed draperies hanging in front of them. These would be like the Frankish mantles worn by Charlemagne, which were twice as long as they were broad and were laid over the left shoulder so that they hung almost to the ground in front and behind, but only to the knee on the left side; they were pinned on the right shoulder, leaving the

Woman's burial, Birka.

Silver brooch showing seated woman; from Hagebyhöga, Gotland.

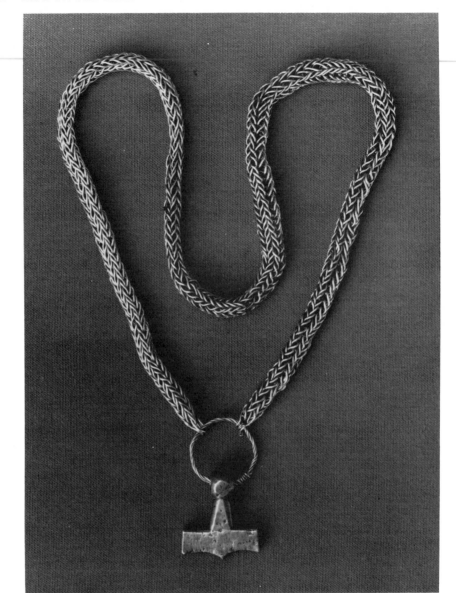

Necklace from Hornelund, Denmark.

Man in long mantle, from a Gotland stone.

edges open on the right side so that the arm was free. Much shorter cloaks, also pinned on the right shoulder, are shown on the Oseberg Tapestry.

Most Viking men wore their hair long enough to cover the neck, and held back by ornamental headbands; others favoured a shorter style with a heavy fringe, to judge by the angry complaint of an eleventh-century Englishman that even in Wessex men were adopting a Danish cut 'with bared neck and blinded eye'. The frequency with which Danes washed their hair also annoyed him, since it made them too attractive to English girls. Most Vikings had moustaches, and often a neatly pointed beard; combs were much in use. Their headgear varied; some caps were round, some pointed, and there were also hoods and broad-brimmed hats. Fur hats were known as 'Russian' hats.

From the sagas we learn that the lower legs were protected by shaped leggings with socks sewn on to them, or sometimes by cloth bands wrapped round the legs. Shoes were of soft leather, those for winter having the hair left on for extra warmth. There was also a very strong kind of primitive boot (such as is called a 'rivlin' in Scotland), which was made of the untanned skin of a cow's hind leg, with the hairy side out and the dewclaws coming on either side of the heel; such footgear is said to be excellent on wet ground and slippery rocks. Hands were protected by mittens or gloves, sometimes of fur.

Besides weaving and making clothes, the other main task of Norse women was cooking and serving meals. There were two main meals in the day; one was fairly early in the morning, probably at about eight or nine, when men had already done about two hours' work; the other was early in the evening and marked the end of the day's work, probably at about seven or eight. The hours must have varied according to local custom and the time of year. Presumably there must also have been short breaks for rest and refreshment in the course of the day, though at what times we do not know.

Several of the basic foods of Iceland required no cooking – the cheeses and *skyr*, for example, or salted meat, or the dried raw fish, which was eaten smeared with butter. But naturally there was also a great deal of cooked meat, fish, porridge, gruel, and bread. The chief drink was ale; mead (from fermented honey) would probably have to be imported from countries further south, and so of course would wine, which was a rare and much-valued luxury.

The surviving cooking vessels are either of metal or of steatite (soapstone). The latter is a most useful material, easy to cut to shape and conveniently fireproof; there are natural outcrops of it in Norway, the Orkneys and Shetlands, and in Greenland, but there are none in Iceland, which therefore had to import vessels of this stone. Both iron and steatite were used for pots and cauldrons, anything up to 18 inches across, with lugs or loops to take an iron handle so that they could hang on chains over a fire. There were also bowls, ladles, saucepans, frying-pans and spits, all of iron or steatite. Pottery was hardly ever used, and what there was of it was mostly imported from the Continent.

Man in baggy trousers, from a Gotland stone.

It must be remembered that great numbers of vessels in wood or leather must have existed; on the rare occasions when soil conditions allow the survival of wooden objects in the graves (as in the Norwegian ship-burials), their variety and high workmanship is most impressive. Such vessels would be more use for storing or serving food than for cooking it, though some methods of cookery – such as slow heating in a bed of ashes – are not impossible with wooden containers; a skin bag, it is said, can be hung over a fire and will not burn so long as the contents are wet.

The hearths of Viking Age houses show that many different cooking methods were employed. Meat could of course be roasted on a spit; it could also be baked in a deep pit filled with embers and covered with earth, and

Soapstone bowl.

Iron cauldron

A grid iron.

this method would also be good for bread. Often the long open hearths had a flat stone slab across one end; this would get very hot, and would be an ideal place for baking bread and oatcakes, and for the slow simmering of stews. The kitchen of the oldest house at Jarlshof had both an open hearth and a stone oven partly built into a wall. There the method was to heat small stones red-hot on the open fire, roll them up a sloping slab into the oven, and cover them with fresh moist grass; the food would be put in, protected by more grass, and covered with another layer of red-hot stones. This particular household cooked much fish in this way; bones of ling, saithe and cod were found in their oven.

It is probable that the piles of small fire-cracked stones to be found near Viking houses show that they followed a primitive method of boiling liquids in wooden vessels by dropping hot stones in, and there are indeed some allusions to this in sagas. Experiment has shown that it only takes half an hour to bring 100 gallons of water to the boil in a wood-lined pit in the ground by this method, and that a ten-pound piece of meat will be stewed in three hours and forty minutes, if the water is kept simmering by adding more stones periodically. However, evidence from Jarlshof and some Scottish sites suggests that sometimes stones had been deliberately broken (by heating them and throwing cold water over them) simply in order to reduce them to convenient sizes; after this they were piled outside the kitchen door, ready for use in a cooking-pit or oven such as has been described.

Meals were eaten in the main room of the house. Here, on the raised flooring that formed a platform along each side of the room, stood various low benches and stools; in wealthy houses, these might be cushioned and covered with draperies, and the flooring would be strewn with straw or rushes. One might also sit directly on this floor itself; an examination of

Fragment of a carved wooden chair, from York.

Icelandic skeletons has shown that women in particular were more used to squatting than to sitting upright. The two places of honour were in the centre of the room, facing each other across the hearth; they were each flanked by two ornate posts called 'high-seat posts'. It has often been assumed that these were the two central pairs of posts holding up the roof, but since they seem to have been detachable (see p. 168) they may have been smaller free-standing objects. The two high-seats were ornate wooden settles, each broad enough to seat at least two people; the first was for the master and mistress of the house, the other for the most honoured guests. All the rest of the household, servants included, sat in two rows along each side of the room, the places near the centre being more honourable than those far out. There were many small low tables, mere boards on trestles, which would be brought in just before the meal and set in front of the people.

Food was served in wooden bowls and dishes, which were carried round by women servants, who also filled the tankards and drinking-horns; if there were guests, the mistress of the house and her daughters might themselves wait upon them. Food was eaten with spoons, knives and fingers; forks were not yet known. Lighting came from steatite lamps filled with whale-oil.

When the meal was ended, the tables would be dismantled and stacked away, and for some while the people would remain sitting round the fires, working at their handicrafts and talking. At length the sleeping-places would be prepared. In houses where there was only one large room, this meant laying out bedding on the same raised floor where the benches had been, though in the more elaborate type of long-house there was a 'sleeping-hall' separate from the 'living-hall', in which bedding could be kept permanently spread. Sometimes, too, a few people might sleep in the kitchen. The raised floors would often have permanent low partitions running from the wall to one of the roof-posts, so that the beds would be laid in shallow, box-like compartments; there are rows of stones crossing the raised floors at Skalakot which may have had this function. The bedding, which by day was kept rolled up out of the way, consisted of a mattress stuffed with straw or hay, bolsters, pillows and quilts stuffed with feathers, rugs, and perhaps an oxhide or sheepskin covering the whole.

The sagas often mention bed-closets built against a wall and entirely enclosed by wooden panelling and lockable doors, which were in effect small private bedrooms for the chief members of the family. Often they were built at one end of the main hall itself; in other cases they were in one or other of the minor rooms. The partitions cutting off one corner of the entrance-hall at Stöng might very well have enclosed a large cupboard-bed of this type. Of cupboards in the modern sense, however, there is no mention; spare clothes must have been stored in chests, and a good many objects were simply hung on pegs in the walls and stacked up in odd corners.

The agricultural life we have been considering has much in common with that of north European peasant communities over many centuries, including some in the British Isles; very many details of house-structure, furnishings, tools and mode of living can find close parallels in Ireland and the Scottish Highlands almost down to our own times. But the Icelandic farmer lived in a world with far wider horizons. He, or his immediate forebears, had pioneered the settlement of new territories, yet he still kept strong links with the old homelands; very likely he would have spent several years of his own youth travelling as a merchant, joining Viking raiding-

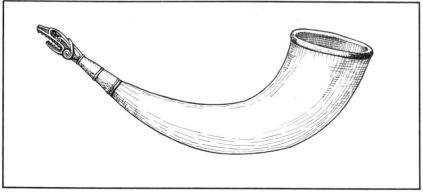

Reconstruction of a drinking horn.

bands, or taking a place in the household of some nobleman or king in Scandinavia, England, or even further afield. The life of a trader or raider was not necessarily closed even to an established farmer with lands of his own, even though it was normally a summer occupation. *The Saga of the Men of Orkney* describes how, as late as 1158, one of their leading men, Svein Asleifsson, still combined farming with the ancient mode of life by plundering:

> At that time it was Svein's custom that he stayed at home in Gairsay all winter, and there he always maintained 80 men at his own cost. He had a drinking hall so large that there was no other as large in the Orkneys. Svein would do much hard work in spring and have great quantities of seed sown, and he would take a great share in this himself. But when this work was ended, he would go a-viking each spring, and would raid the Scottish Isles and Ireland, and he would come home at midsummer. This he called 'spring viking'. Then he would stay at home till the cornfields had been reaped and the grain dealt with. Then he would go a-viking, and not come back till one month of the winter was over, and this he called 'autumn viking'.

4
Ships and Seafaring

The history of the Vikings is intimately linked with their emergence as masters of the seas. Trading ventures, piracy, coastal raids, the long voyages of the settlers – all were made possible by the technical achievements of shipwrights and seamen whose skill was unequalled in Europe. Their ships were the culmination of several centuries of development, the stages in which can be studied in ancient rock-carving, in certain pre-Viking ships from bogs and burial-mounds, and from pictures on the carved stones of Gotland. The crucial developments were the discovery and increasing size of the sail, the perfecting of the characteristic rudder placed upon the starboard side near the stern, and the evolution of a true keel of great strength. By the late eighth century, Viking vessels were capable of direct crossings of the North Sea, and the startled West found itself confronted by raiders whose very coming was a matter for amazement.

Viking ships were designed to serve many different purposes, and so were by no means all of the same size and type. The three that are the best known and best preserved come from Norwegian burial-mounds that lie round the Oslo Fjord, at Gokstad, Oseberg and Tune; three rowing-boats accompanied the Gokstad ship; five other large ships, of a later period, were raised in 1962 from the Roskilde Fjord in Denmark. All these vessels (together with many others, less well preserved, of which remains have been found in various burial-places) show a basic similarity in structure; but they also show marked variations, so that it is clear that among both warships and merchant ships numerous specialized types had been evolved. This is confirmed by the number of different names applied to ships in written sources.

Of the three Norwegian ships, that from Gokstad has contributed the most to our picture of a typical Viking vessel of the ninth century, although it is smaller than those built in later centuries. It was found in 1880 in a burial-mound, embedded in a thick layer of blue clay which had preserved its woodwork almost intact; it had served for the burial of a strongly built man of middle age, and this burial probably dates from about 900.

The Gokstad ship is 76 feet 6 inches long from the tip of the prow to the stern; the keel is shaped from a single piece of oak, from which the stem and stern rise in elegant and sharply profiled curves. Only their topmost peaks are missing, rotted away because they protruded above the protective layer

The Gokstad ship.

of clay into the ordinary earth of the mound. The hull is formed of 16 strakes; it is 17 feet 6 inches in the beam, and 6 ft 5 inches deep amidships; it would draw about three foot in the water. The ship is clinker-built, each strake overlapping that below and riveted to it; in most strakes the planking is no more than one inch thick, but in the tenth, which is at the waterline, and in the fourteenth, which has the oarholes, it has been left slightly thicker to bear the extra strain. The gunwale is very sturdy. All grooves and joints have been caulked with plugs of animal hair and wool woven together in a loose cord.

The internal structure of the ship is formed by 19 ribs, three feet apart, on which rest crossbeams; below the waterline the planking of the hull is not nailed to these ribs but lashed to them, the lashings being made of spruce-roots, and passing through cleats left in the planks when they were cut into shape. This technique ensured that the ship would be supple enough to ride heavy seas without parting; had the structure been rigid, the timbers would have had to be far thicker to stand the strain, and all the advantages of lightness and speed would have been lost. In some areas of Scandinavia lashings were apparently used even more extensively than on the Gokstad ship, for we are told that in the winter of 1138–9 Sigurd Slembidjakn (a claimant to the throne of Norway) got some Lapland shipwrights to build two boats for him, 'and they were fastened together with deer sinews, without nails, and with withies of willow instead of knees, and each boat could carry 12 men'.

The Gokstad ship does not have a fixed deck; its floorboards are of pine, and rest loosely on the crossbeams without being fastened down in any way. They could be lifted at any point, so that bilgewater could be easily bailed out, or items stored beneath the boards could be reached. Bailing-scoops have been found on board this and other ships, and buckets were also used; pumps were unknown.

Probably the strangest feature of a Viking ship, to the modern eye, is its rudder, but this is in fact one of their outstanding technical achievements. It

The wagon from the Oseberg ship.

is shaped like a very broad and massive oar-blade mounted on the starboard quarter, and when in its normal position it projects some 18 inches below the line of the keel, providing a good lateral resistance to the water. Yet the depth of the rudder is readily adjustable in shallow water. Its main point of attachment is a block of oak which is made fast, through the planking, to a specially strengthened rib; its secondary attachment is by a strap that holds it to the gunwale, and if the steersman releases this strap and at the same time hauls in a rope attached to the bottom end of the rudder, the latter will swivel round on the pivot formed by the oak block, and will thus be raised clear of the bottom. The tiller is detachable; that of the Gokstad ship is over a yard long, and is embellished with a finely carved animal head.

The Gokstad ship was designed for rowing or for sailing. The mast is of pine, almost a foot thick, and was stepped into a heavy block of oak, 12 feet long, that rests along the bottom of the ship; above this, resting on the crossbeams, is an even longer block that served to steady the mast, and had a slit cut through it to allow the mast to be raised and lowered. The total height of the mast is uncertain, for part of it had been cut off and laid flat along the deck, so that it should not stick up out of the mound, and part too has rotted; probably it was about 30 feet high. A heap of whitish woollen cloth, striped with red and entangled with fragments of hempen rope, is all that remains of the sail.

Along each side of the ship there are 16 oarholes, each with a small slit radiating from it to take the blade of the oar as it was passed through from the inside of the ship; each hole also has a small round shutter on the inside, to keep it watertight when the ship was under sail. The oars are of pine, varying in length from about 17 to about 19 feet, so that all of them would strike the water together, in spite of the rising curve of the ship's lines. The oars are very light, and have slender tapering blades. When not in use, they, together with the various spars, would be stacked on T-shaped supports that

Tiller of the Gokstad ship.

rose seven feet above the deck, well out of the way of men moving to and fro. One thing that is not clear about the rowing arrangements is the actual position of the oarsmen; no rowing benches were found, yet the height of the oarholes relative to the floorboards seems to rule out the possibility that the rowers remained standing. It has been suggested that they sat on their sea-chests, and that no such chests were found in the buried ship because they were the personal property of the seamen, not part of the ship's own fittings.

Above the row of oarholes, just below the gunwale, was fixed a light rail, and from this were hung shields, all along the outside of the ship. There are 64 of them, 32 on each side, and they are painted alternately black and yellow; they were hung in such a way that each partly overlapped its neighbour, and each pair corresponded to one oarhole. From passages in sagas it appears that shields were thus displayed when ships lay in harbour, and sometimes also as warships sailed in to the attack; but they certainly could not have been left there when on the open seas, for they were only lightly fastened and the first strong wave would have carried them away.

The whole beauty of the Gokstad ship is sober and functional, the beauty of clean, strong lines and superbly calculated construction. Decorative carving is kept to the minimum – some lightly incised lines on the floorboards and oarhole-shutters, the animal head upon the tiller, and presumably an animal head or other ornament to crown the lost peaks of the prow and stern. Traces of a simple and effective colour-scheme survive; the black and yellow of the shields is echoed in lines of paint on the animal head of the tiller, where touches of red can also be seen, and these same three colours recur on the carved animal-headed framework of the ship's tent, and in the blankets and quilt of the bed on which the owner's corpse was laid. The figurehead would probably have matched the other carvings in style and colouring, and the whole scheme, like a simple heraldic device, would serve to identify the ship and her owner.

In striking contrast to the Gokstad ship is the lavish richness of the vessel found at Oseberg in 1903. The general structure is similar, its length is only a few feet less, it has only one less pair of oars, and its breadth is almost the same; yet the total impression is most unlike, for it is not even three feet deep amidships, and from its long, low sides the prow and stern spring high above the water, the soaring curves of the prow ending in the spiral of a coiling snake. Bands of rich carving outline the two edges of both sides of the prow with a pattern of sinuous scrolls, which on close inspection resolve themselves into rows of intertwining beasts. Anyone standing on deck and facing the prow would see another panel of carving, more grotesque and humorous in style, where small semi-human figures with goggle eyes and tadpole bodies clutch and clamber over one another.

Yet the Oseberg ship, richly worked as it is, can never have been meant to sail the open seas. It lies vulnerably low in the water, its keel is thin, its oarholes lack shutters, there are weak areas in stern and hull caused by joins in the planking, and its floorboards are almost all nailed down, so that in an emergency bailing would be nearly impossible. Such a craft would only be suited to the calm waters of a sheltered fjord; it must have been designed for pleasure cruising, or possibly, since several objects found with it may well have religious associations, it may have been used in the cult of some deity. It is perhaps also relevant that the bodies found in it were those of two women.

The burial took place towards the middle of the ninth century, but the ship was already old and worn when it was laid in the mound. Its keel was rather battered, and the mast-block had split and been repaired; the tiller was missing; the oars, rudder and mast seem to be replacements rather than the original fittings – indeed, several oars have not even been completed.

One of four carved animal-headed posts found in the Oseberg ship.

The Oseberg ship.

Carving on the prow of the
Oseberg ship.

Apparently the ship had been out of use for some years and had been stripped of part of its equipment, so that it had to be hastily fitted out once more to make it worthy of its final task.

The third Norwegian ship is that from Tune, unearthed in 1867, and not nearly so well preserved as the two others. It is of about the same period as the Gokstad ship (*c*.900). Its dimensions were probably about 65 feet long, 14 feet 6 inches in the beam, and 4 feet 5 inches deep amidships, but in cross-section it is much more flat-bottomed than the Gokstad ship, and the two broad strakes above the waterline are strongly slanted outwards. It has sturdy mast-blocks, and probably had ten or eleven pairs of oars; the low, broad hull must have made it very stable, and its shallow draught would suit it for use in estuaries or among shoals.

The seaworthiness of Viking ships was proved beyond a doubt in 1893, when an exact replica of the Gokstad ship was sailed across the Atlantic by Captain Magnus Andersen; she left Norway on 30 April and reached Newfoundland on 27 May, having encountered several storms without damage, and having achieved maximum speeds of 10 or 11 knots under sail. The captain expressed the utmost praise for her elasticity and lightness, and for the suppleness with which, in heavy seas, her timbers would play to meet the strain; he also declared that the side-rudder made for very easy and efficient steering.

It was usually believed that Viking ships, because of their square sails, could only be sailed before the wind; Captain Andersen therefore fitted his vessel with a staysail, though this was unknown in the Viking Age. Since then, however, a closer study of the Gokstad ship has shown that in fact the sail's foot could be extended by a boom wedged into a certain socket on the deck; this device, possibly aided by a bowline, would enable the ship to sail near the wind, and even to tack. It was adopted by a later replica of the Gokstad ship built in 1949, which by this means was able to sail close-hauled within $5\frac{1}{2}$–6 points of the wind.

What rigging a Viking ship would carry is uncertain, especially since the top of the Gokstad mast is missing and therefore one cannot tell whether there were holes through which a backstay could be passed. On the whole it seems likely that stays and shrouds were used, and that a pair of wooden blocks found in the ship served to keep them tense. The yard on which the sail was hoisted is incomplete, but was probably some 33 feet long.

The picture-stones of Gotland show very many representations of ships in full sail, which raise interesting problems. Stays and bowlines are sometimes included, sometimes not. The sails themselves are usually covered with a diamond-shaped pattern, whereas written sources speak of sails having vertical stripes in contrasting colours. Either the Gotlanders preferred a different pattern, or, more probably, the diamond shapes represent a network of ropes or leather thongs which covered the surface of the loosely woven sail to strengthen it; pieces of rope entangled in the remains of the Gokstad ship's sail could well be fragments of such a network.

The Gotland pictures also show curious criss-cross lines hanging from the foot of the sail and held by members of the crew; sometimes these lines seem to prolong the network on the sail itself, but more usually they look like a separate set of ropes looped round the lower yard. They may well be sheet-lines to swing the lower yard and trim the sail; or they may be reefing lines running through loops sewn upon the sail itself and used for raising and lowering it fast and evenly, in which case the stone pictures may represent the moment when the sail has just been lowered at the beginning of the voyage.

Ships normally carried one or more small boats as dinghies, towing them, or stowing them on deck. Three such were found at Gokstad, the largest being a graceful clinker-built boat over 30 feet long, with three pairs of oars working in delicately carved rowlocks. Another of them, 21 feet long and with two pairs of oars, has recently been the subject of an interesting experiment at the National Maritime Museum, Greenwich. A replica, constructed by techniques known to have been available in the Viking Age, underwent rowing trials in various sea conditions, with great success; the only reservation concerned the typical Viking side-rudder, which made it difficult to change course quickly. The researchers judged it 'potentially a splendid craft for mackerel spinning, but not suitable for bringing a large lively fish on a line in over the side'. A boat like this may serve to remind us of the many small, light craft which must have been used on lakes and rivers, and for the fishing expeditions and other short coastal journeys of daily life. It is usually these small boats that have left their traces in the hundreds of Norwegian ship-burials.

Ships also carried tents, and frames for these were found both at Gokstad and at Oseberg. They were made of ash, and the boards which formed the gables at each end were carved into animal heads that would protrude above the fabric, their fierce features warding off evil from the sleepers; those at Gokstad were painted in the ship's colours, yellow, black and red. The frames of dismantled beds were also found, some with animal heads closely matching those of the tent-frames; clearly, the tents and beds had formed a set. The tents were very roomy; at Oseberg one is 17 feet 3 inches long, 14 feet 7 inches broad, and 11 feet 5 inches high, while the other is only slightly less long and broad and is 8 feet 9 inches high. Such tents were sometimes pitched on deck when the ship was moored, but more often, on coastal voyages, the men would go ashore each night and pitch tent on land. Those for whom there were no beds would use sleeping-bags of hide, often sharing them for warmth.

A night on shore gave opportunity for cooking. Kitchen gear found in the Oseberg ship included two iron cauldrons with their chains and pothooks, spoons, knives, axes, wooden bowls, tubs and dishes, and a handmill for grinding corn; the carcass of an ox was laid out upon two boards. At Gokstad there was a huge bronze cauldron and many wooden dishes, chopping boards, kegs, cups, bowls and ladles; even two candlesticks were found. In other buried or burnt ships whose wooden equipment has perished, the

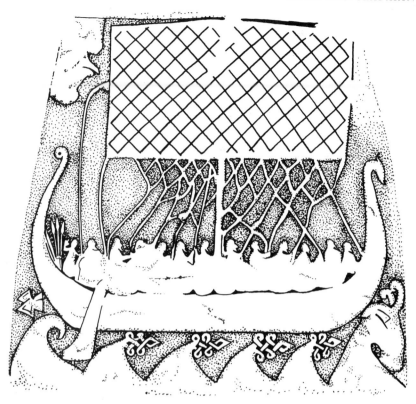

A ship in full sail; detail from a Gotland stone.

Rowing boats found with the Gokstad ship.

Tent-frame, found in the
Gokstad ship.

Kitchen gear found in the
Oseberg ship.

cauldron at least is almost always to be found. Of course, the objects found in a ship-burial include not only the ship's own fittings but also many possessions brought from the dead man's home, but it is obvious that good cooking gear must have been a regular part of any ship's equipment. It is even possible that cooking might be done at sea during the longer voyages, using a large box well packed with sand to hold a fire in safety. In any case there would also be provisions requiring no cooking: dried fish, smoked meats, hard-baked bread, fruit, nuts, casks of cheesy curds and sour butter, and barrels of ale and mead. An interesting recent find in Dublin casts further light on how Vikings solved the problem of transporting liquids on board ship. It is a broad-based wooden container, its lid pierced by a central hole that is closed by a swivelling cover; an inward-sloping spout ensures that no liquid can escape unless the container is deliberately lifted and held upside down.

It is not to be supposed, however, that all long voyages over the open seas were achieved in vessels exactly like that from Gokstad. Merchants with bulky cargoes of timber or bales of cloth, settlers with their livestock, even raiders such as those who in 893 shipped their horses from France to England – all needed heavier ships with greater room for stowage, of broader and higher build. Many sagas allude to such vessels, but until recently the only concrete trace of one was a massive 13-foot rudder from Rebaek in Denmark. Then, in 1962, a barrage of sunken wrecks in a channel of Roskilde Fjord was examined, and found to consist of five ships from the eleventh century. One is undoubtedly the most massive ship yet found in Scandinavia, almost 88 feet long, very broad, and sturdily built of thick pinewood planking that could defy the heaviest seas. This vessel, known as Wreck 1, had a roomy hold amidships and was only decked fore-and-aft; it would be well suited to carry large cargoes and even livestock on long open-sea voyages. Wreck 2 was an oaken warship, so badly broken up by currents that at first it was thought to be two separate ships; it is now seen to be a true 'longship', 144 feet long, that could carry 60 warriors. Wreck 3, like Wreck 1, was a merchant ship, but a smaller, lighter one; it too had an open hold and two half-decks, and oarholes only at the half-decks. This ship may well be typical of the many small merchant craft used in Baltic waters. Wreck 4 is a rather battered warship, of the same general type as the Gokstad ship. Finally, there is a flat-bottomed craft, of pinewood, without oarholes, and with a remarkably slender mast; this may well be some form of ferryboat for use in estuaries and shallow, sheltered waters.

The most famous Viking ships were, naturally, those of the raiding fleets that harried England and the Continent, the 'longships' and 'dragon-ships'. At first, in King Alfred's time, they apparently were hardly larger than the Gokstad ship with its 16 pairs of oars, to judge by one famous passage in the *Anglo-Saxon Chronicle*. This describes how Alfred designed ships 'some with 60 oars and some with more' to combat the raiders, and says these English ships 'were very nearly twice as long as the others', thus implying that Viking vessels had about 30 to 40 oars (15 to 20 pairs).

Thus it seems that the ninth-century Viking warship was fairly small, but in succeeding centuries their vessels – at least those of kings and nobles – grew ever larger and more splendid. In descriptions referring to the eleventh century, ships with 25, 30 and 35 pairs of oars are mentioned. Such ships are typified by the famous *Long Serpent*, built for King Olaf Tryggvason in the winter of 999–1000. According to Snorri's account, it had 34 pairs of oars, and the flat part of the keel alone was almost 110 feet long, excluding stem and stern. When it was fully manned for battle, eight men sat at each oar and 30 stood in the prow, making 574 men aboard in all. Such figures seem hardly credible, and have almost certainly been inflated by legend; more reasonable are the figures given in connection with later medieval ship-levies, which demanded three men to each oar – one to row, one to shield the rower, and one for actual fighting. Certainly raiders crossing the North Sea would never risk crowding their ships so thickly.

A merchant ship: reconstruction of Wreck I, from Skuldelev, Roskilde Fjord.

Nor is it certain how many ships might make up an average raiding fleet. Figures given in chronicles are often very large, but may be suspected of exaggeration; nor do they distinguish between large warships and the lesser boats that accompanied them. A fair example, reliably recorded, would be the fleet with which Olaf Tryggvason set sail to attack Wendland in 1000; he had 60 ships, of which at least 14 had 30 pairs of oars or more, others had 20, and the rest were 'small craft and provision vessels'. When Harald Hardradi invaded England in 1066, his fleet was of 200 warships, plus smaller craft.

But, even if the numbers of the fleets were not so overwhelming as some chronicles would suggest, there can be no doubt of the terror which the sight of them inspired. A Latin text describes the fleet which Cnut brought to England in 1015:

So great also was the ornamentation of the ships that the eyes of the beholders were dazzled, and to those looking from afar they seemed to be of flame rather than of wood. For if at any time the sun cast the splendour of his rays among them, the flashing of arms shone in one place, and in another the flame of suspended shields. Gold shone on the prows, silver also flashed on the variously-shaped ships. So great, in fact, was the magnificence of the fleet, that if its lord had desired to conquer any peoples, the ships alone would have terrified the enemy, before the warriors whom they carried joined battle at all. For who could look upon the lions of the foe, terrible with the brightness of gold, who upon the men of metal, menacing with golden face, who upon the bulls on the ships, threatening death, their horns shining with gold – without feeling any fear for the king of such a force?

The shields, the painting and the gilding are characteristic of the warships; so too are the animal or human figureheads, from which came the general term 'dragon-ships' and also names of individual ships: *Long Serpent*, *Bison*, *Crane*, *Man's Head*. Animal figureheads have a long history in Scandinavia; the early Gotland stones show ships with horse-headed prows, while later ones are snake-like. Carved posts with gaping monsters' heads dredged from the Scheldt are probably figureheads of small ships, and are thought to be earlier than the Viking Age; other such posts were found in the burial-chamber on board the Oseberg ship, though it is not known to what sort of object they had originally been attached. The snake figurehead of the Oseberg ship itself is a fixed part of the structure, but we know from other sources that figureheads usually could be detached. Icelandic law states that this must be done on nearing the coast, lest the good spirits of the land should take fright; on the Bayeux Tapestry William's fleet is seen sailing with figureheads, but the same ships, when beached, are mostly shown as headless.

Another characteristic of the later warships was a weather-vane of gilded bronze, richly adorned with animal figures and scroll-work. Several fine eleventh-century examples have survived because they had been bestowed on churches, presumably in thanksgiving for safe voyages. It is not certain

A weather-vane from a Swedish church, believed to have originally belonged to a late Viking Age ship.

where these vanes were placed on the ship; the masthead would seem the most natural spot, but the fine detailed metalwork would be invisible at such a height, so a shaft set up on deck or even the prow itself is perhaps more likely. Several vanes are scored and dented, perhaps by arrows that struck them in battle.

As regards the technique of the shipwrights, study of the surviving ships tells much. Experience in building replicas, as is now increasingly done in both Scandinavian and English museums, will greatly increase our understanding of the techniques involved. At the conclusion of one such experiment at the National Maritime Museum, the researchers declared their judgement on the boatbuilders of the Viking Age: '[They] cannot be faulted on any major point: they achieved a near optimal solution.'

Shipbuilding was winter work – necessarily so for the farmer making his own fishing or trading vessel in the season when work on the land was ended, but apparently also for the specialist craftsmen who built the royal warships. Timber would sometimes be chosen and felled many months in advance, roughly cut to shape, and stored in marshy pools to keep it supple till enough was ready to start work on the ship. There were, however, advantages in unseasoned oak, the use of which was also very common. In the Viking Age Norway was rich in oak forests, but centuries of shipbuilding took such toll that it was with great difficulty that a native oak was found to make the mast-block of the 1893 replica of the Gokstad ship, and her keel timber had to be brought from Canada. However, recent study of the Roskilde Fjord ships indicates that Viking shipbuilders were skilled enough to scarf keels, so that it was not after all essential to make the keel from a single piece of wood. It was also at one time thought that only two planks could be extracted from each log, the log being split once through the middle and each half then chopped to shape with axes and adzes; but as in fact the planks have a wedge-shaped profile they must have been produced by the far less wasteful process of repeated splitting along the radii of the log – like cutting wedges from a round cake. Furthermore, radial planks are stronger, and less inclined to shrink if fashioned from unseasoned timber.

Many men were employed in building a large ship such as the *Long Serpent*, 'some to fell wood, some to shape it, some to make nails, some to carry timber'. Her keel was laid out on stocks, traces of which could still be seen 200 years later when Snorri wrote; stem and stern were riveted on, and the side planking followed. At this stage the master-builder, Thorberg, happened to be called away and did not return till the planking was complete on both sides of the hull. Everyone, including King Olaf, was very pleased with the work; but next day the king found all the carpenters standing idle and saying the ship was ruined, for in the night someone had gone from stem to stern hacking one deep notch after another along the planking of one side. Thorberg had done this himself; when Olaf threatened him with death if he did not repair the damage, he did so not by putting new planking in but by paring the wood away until all was smoothed down to the level of the notches. The result pleased the king so much that Thorberg was asked to do the same on the other side of the hull. The story shows how greatly the Norsemen valued thinness and lightness in a ship's timbers, and the fame won by a craftsman who had the bold confidence to pare off the least unnecessary fraction of an inch.

It was not merely the Viking ships themselves that amazed the rest of Europe, but also the voyages they accomplished. Most seamen were only capable of coastal navigation, steering from one known landmark to the next; the Scandinavians naturally used this method too (as can be seen from the story of the Norwegian trader Ohthere, Chapter 5), but they also made direct crossings of the North Sea and of wide stretches of the Atlantic. The sagas give less information than one would wish about how such crossings were accomplished, speaking of them with a casual brevity which in itself shows how much they were a normal, everyday affair to all the Scandinavians. Yet they do contain some valuable hints, and these are supplemented by the practical experience of modern seamen who have studied the Viking ships and sailed in replicas of them.

There was nothing haphazard about Viking navigation. It is true that traditional accounts of the finding of new lands – Iceland, Greenland,

America – ascribe the first discovery in each case to an accidental sighting by a ship driven off course by a storm, or drifting in a fog. But in each case the discoverer, disliking the look of his new-found land, made his way back home, and it was only later that others deliberately set out, on the basis of the information he had brought, to explore and settle the new regions. How then, in an age when the magnetic compass was unknown, did these following explorers set their course? And how, from then on, did continuous streams of ships ply to and fro between Norway and Iceland, Iceland and Greenland, and even directly across vast stretches of ocean between Norway and Greenland?

To some extent, the observation of landmarks was still possible: thus a later medieval text gives instructions for the Greenland course:

> From Hernar in Norway set sail due west for Hvarf in Greenland. You are to sail to the north of Shetland in such a way that you can just sight it in clear weather; but to the south of the Faroes, in such a way that the sea seems to be half way up the mountain slopes; and steer south of Iceland, in such a way that you can sight birds and whales from there.

Mountain peaks would certainly be useful landmarks in clear weather, and even when the land itself was below the horizon there would be certain signs to show its direction – cloud formations, the reflected light which icefields cast into the sky, the presence of certain species of seabirds, and their lines of flight. It may be that the settler who released two ravens to guide him to land was not acting simply out of piety to Odin, but on the practical grounds that a hungry raven, flying high, will head for land which men at sea-level cannot yet see.

Yet such observations could only be made in favourable conditions, and were in any case irrelevant to the long ocean crossings, far out of reach of any land. Here the key principle of navigation was latitude sailing, as can be seen in the sailing instructions just quoted; those making for Greenland are not to set out from any part of the Norwegian coast, but from a point some 30 miles north of Bergen, which lies on the same latitude as an area on the west coast of Greenland, about 80 miles north of its southern tip. If they could hold their course steadily upon the same latitude, they were sure to reach their goal.

The Norsemen clearly understood the relation between the sun's maximum height at noon and the latitude of the place from which the observation was made, could calculate it accurately, and could even make

Prows of a Viking fleet; wood carving from Bergen.

allowance for its seasonal variation. There exists an Icelandic set of tables giving the sun's midday height for every week through the year, as observed in northern Iceland; it is ascribed to a man nicknamed Star-Oddi, and dates from the early eleventh century. These remarkably accurate calculations are expressed in units called 'half-wheels', i.e. half the apparent diameter of the sun. A man holding at arm's length a stick marked off in these or any other convenient units could record the sun's height in any place where he might find himself, and so estimate the latitude by comparison with that of other places known to him. If need be, he could use cruder methods, such as measuring a shadow cast at noon. Or he could use the stars, as did an Icelander on pilgrimage to Palestine in about 1150, who reported that the latitude of the Jordan was such that when he lay flat on his back on the bank, raised one knee, and placed his fist on his knee with the thumb pointing upwards, then the Pole Star would appear exactly at the tip of his thumb, and no higher. It is in fact easier to make such calculations by the Pole Star than by the sun, but in northern latitudes during the summer months the night sky is too bright for stars to be visible.

One can therefore assume that when a Viking sighted an unknown land he would calculate its latitude, and that those who followed him would not have to sail vaguely westward into the blue in the hope of finding it again, but would know how far to the north or south it lay. Daily checks would ensure that the sun's midday height remained the same. If they met with storms or fog, they would be helpless as long as the sun was hidden, but as soon as they could resume their observations they would know that if it now stood higher in the sky they were too far south; if lower, too far north. They had no way of telling how far west or east they might have been driven, but this was a comparatively minor matter; if they returned to the right latitude and then turned west they were bound sooner or later to reach the point for which they had set out.

To guide their steering they must have used a bearing-dial by which to establish the points of the compass by reference to the sun – or to the Pole Star, if this were visible. Old Norse contains names for eight points of the compass; those for NE and SE are 'landnorth' and 'landsouth', and those for NW and SW are 'outnorth' and 'outsouth', the 'out-' meaning 'out to sea'. The system must have been evolved by seamen on a route where long stretches of land lay to the east, and open sea to the west, as would be the case along the coasts of Norway. The language has no special terms for subdivisions such as NNE, which must mean that the oldest dials would have had eight points only.

But in 1948 a half of a notched disk of wood was found in Greenland, in ruins probably of the fourteenth century. If the disk had been complete, the notches would amount to 32; this corresponds to a 32-point division of the horizon known to have been used in the late Middle Ages, and it has therefore been suggested that Norse seamen used a more refined bearing-system than had been suspected, and that this object is one of their bearing-dials. It has a hole in the centre which would take a shaft as handle, and such a shaft might also hold a shadow-pin and a movable pointer to mark the course, which would be useful, though not essential. Two particular notches at right angles to one another seem to be emphasized by certain scratches; they would stand for two of the cardinal points, perhaps north and west.

To take a bearing with this dial (or with a cruder one of eight or 16 points), the seaman need only turn it till the notch representing the south pointed to the spot where a vertical line drawn from the midday sun would cut the horizon; he would then see all other points of the compass at a glance, and could alter course till the ship's prow lay in line with the notch marking the desired direction. By night, if the Pole Star was visible, he could align the northern notch upon it. If he knew by experience at what precise point the sun would rise at the season of his journey, he would not need to wait till noon but could take bearings at dawn by aligning the correct notch upon the rising sun; he might even have tables to help him make this reckoning, for Star-Oddi composed seasonal tables for this, as well as those for the sun's midday altitude.

It seems possible too that some men knew how to find the sun's position on a cloudy day by scanning the sky through a piece of Iceland spar, which has the natural property of polarizing light, for certain sagas mention a 'sun-stone' used for this purpose. Tourmaline, which can be found in the Oslo Fjord area, is another stone with the same property; pieces of it, and also of Iceland spar, have been found in Viking ship-burials. Experiment has shown that in misty weather such a 'sun-stone' changes colour from pink to pale blue when it is held towards the direction of the hidden sun – a crude but useful guide to anyone caught in a sea-fog.

By the skill of their navigators and the craftsmanship of their shipwrights the Norsemen were masters of the seas, and their bold sailing-directions ring out confidently down the ages: 'From Hernar in Norway set sail due west for Greenland. . . .'

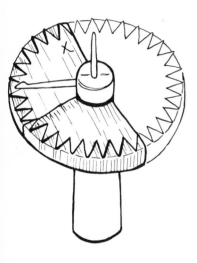

Reconstruction of a bearing-dial found in Greenland.

5
The Merchants

The warlike reputation of the Scandinavians has often obscured the fact that much of their wealth was undoubtedly acquired by trade – a trade based partly on the natural resources of their own lands, though also on goods exacted as tribute from neighbouring races, and on slaves seized by force. Wealth of the first two kinds is well illustrated by the story of a Norwegian chieftain from Halogaland who visited the court of King Alfred some time in the 870s, and whose account of his homeland and journeys was incorporated into an Anglo-Saxon translation of Orosius' *History of the World*. The Anglo-Saxon form of his name is Ohthere, corresponding to Norse Ottar; he did a little farming, bred reindeer, hunted whales and walrus, took tribute from the Lapps, and was evidently also a merchant:

> He was a very wealthy man in the goods in which their wealth consists, that is, wild deer. At the time when he visited the king he had 720 tamed deer still unsold; they call these deer 'reindeer'. Six of them were decoy deer, which are very expensive among the Lapps because they catch the wild deer with them. He was among the chief men of that land, although he had no more than 20 oxen and 20 sheep and 20 swine, and what little he ploughed, he ploughed with horses. But their riches mainly consist in the tribute which the Lapps pay them; this tribute is of animals' skins, birds' feathers, walrus ivory, and ship-ropes that are made from hides of walrus or seals. Every man pays according to his birth; the most nobly-born must pay 15 marten skins, and five walrus hides, and one bearskin, and ten measures of feathers, and a kirtle of bearskin or otter-skin, and two ship-ropes; each of these must by 60 ells long and made from the hide either of walrus or seal.

Ohthere described two of his voyages. In the first he went north along the Norwegian coast, beyond the northernmost whaling-grounds, then eastwards along coasts where only nomad tribes lived, and so reached the White Sea. It was, he said, a voyage of exploration 'to find out how far the land continued to the north-east, and whether anyone lived to the north of that waste'; but he also went 'for the sake of the walrus, as they have very fine ivory in their tusks – he brought some of these tusks to the king – and their hide is very good for ship-ropes.' It is tempting to wonder whether his subsequent arrival in England was an attempt to find a new market for the goods he praises so much; certainly there was a demand for both. Walrus and seal ropes (made by cutting the beast's hide in a single continuous strip in a spiral from shoulders to tail) were indeed very strong; as for walrus ivory, it was a fine substitute for elephant ivory, both for ecclesiastical objects such as crucifixes and croziers, and for secular ones such as caskets and sword-grips. Blubber-oil for lamps must have been a useful though prosaic by-product of this trade.

However, Ohthere was certainly not unique in taking an interest in these Arctic regions, for archaeological finds show that Norwegians were very active there both before and after his time; sagas, too, tell of the rich skin-trade of the far north, and the anger of the local chieftains when Harald Fairhair demanded that the Lappish tribute should be a royal monopoly. It may even be that England became a regular market for Arctic produce; *Egil's Saga* tells how Thorolf Kveldulfsson, also from Halogaland, brought a shipload of furs and dried fish to England and traded them for honey, wheat, wine and cloth.

The second voyage Ohthere described was one which he must surely have made many times, setting out from Halogaland and sailing south down the coast of Norway:

> There is a market-town [*port*] in the south of that land, which is called *Sciringes Heal*. He said one could sail there in a month, if one camped ashore by night and had a favourable wind every day, and all the while one would be sailing along land. . . . To the south of *Sciringes Heal* a very great sea [the Skagerak] cuts into the land; it is broader than any man can see over. . . . And he said that in five days he sailed from *Sciringes Heal* to the market-town which men called *aet Haeðum*; it stands between the Wends and the Saxons and the Angles, and belongs to the Danes.

The place-names here given in Anglo-Saxon forms correspond to Skiringssal and Hedeby; the latter has long been known as a major trading centre at the base of the Jutland peninsula, while the former is a small district on the west side of the Oslo Fjord, where the actual market has recently been identified at a little village called Kaupang. Excavations at these spots have proved how well known was the route followed by Ohthere.

Kaupang lies at the head of a small bay which forms an excellent harbour, and is protected from seaborne raids by the maze of islets and shallow channels at the mouth; it has no fortifications on the landward side, probably because the high mountains behind were reckoned protection enough. At the foot of these stood some scattered buildings; between them and the shore lies a wide, sloping meadow, on which visiting traders may well have pitched their tents. We know from sagas that neither the Norwegian merchants who sailed to Iceland nor the local farmers needed permanent buildings at the trading-centres; all they had were roofless turf-walled 'booths', repaired and tented over when a ship came in. It is too soon to say whether this was also the case at Kaupang, for the settlement area is still being excavated, and more houses may yet be discovered.

In the surrrounding region there are many graves whose contents show contacts between Kaupang and countries to the south and west: Frankish glass, Rhineland pottery, and many objects from the British Isles. The latter should not necessarily be thought of as raiders' booty; the stories of Ohthere and Thorolf show that good relations could exist between Norwegians and Englishmen, even in Wessex, while the fact that until late in the tenth century most English coins found in Norway were from the York and Chester mints probably points to trade between Norway and the Viking settlements in northern England. As for Irish objects in Norway, it has been noticed that those from the early Viking Age are, typically, broken reliquaries or book-clasps roughly adapted as ornaments or harness mounts, their brutal treatment speaking eloquently of looters' ways; by contrast, in the late ninth and tenth centuries Norway was obtaining many delicate Celtic objects of thin tin-bronze (bowls, small buckets, elegant scales and weights), in such perfect condition that they must surely have been transported under the care of merchants whose profits depended on their safe handling of these fragile wares.

Men who came down to Kaupang from the far north would certainly have found wealthy men there to buy their Arctic luxuries; only a few miles away are the lavish ship-burials of Oseberg and Gokstad, and many other well-furnished graves show how rich the whole region was. Other traders, like Ohthere himself, might wish to take their goods south to Hedeby; it has been suggested that these men gathered at Kaupang before sailing in convoy, for mutual protection in the pirate-haunted seas off eastern Jutland.

From this centre too the men of southern Norway could set out for the Continent with their own type of wares – iron goods, birds' feathers and down, timber, honey, perhaps dried fish (though it is disputed whether the Norwegian fisheries were commercially exploited as early as this), and certainly the products of the steatite quarries, which were numerous in this area. Steatite (soapstone) was much used for loom-weights, spindle-whorls, lamps, bowls, cooking-pots, and moulds for metal casting; it had the advantages of being soft to cut and highly fireproof. There was rarely any need to dig pits or galleries to reach it, for the natural outcrops formed good vertical faces, from which objects could be fashioned in the living rock. Using long chisels, the worker would rough out from the rock the outer shape of, say, a bowl, making it rather larger than the eventual size, and having the base outermost; he would then undercut, forming a sort of mushroom, till he could break it off. Then he would hollow out the inside, shape the surfaces with a finer chisel, and scour it smooth. Often the final processes would be carried out at home, and at the foot of some rock-faces there still lie unfinished bowls which were never carried away. Steatite vessels were sent in large numbers to other parts of Norway, to Denmark, to Germany, and to Iceland; Kaupang must have been an important centre for this trade. It is presumably due to the popularity of steatite vessels that native Scandinavian pottery is hardly to be found until late in the Viking Age.

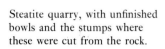

Steatite quarry, with unfinished bowls and the stumps where these were cut from the rock.

Men cutting up a whale, from a codex of Icelandic laws (*Jónsbók*, fourteenth century).

From Kaupang Ohthere went to Hedeby, one of the most flourishing towns of northern Europe, being placed as it was at the junction of several major trade-routes. It was on a lake at the head of the navigable river Schlei, at the base of the Jutland peninsula; less than a dozen miles to the west was Hollingsted on the river Treene, equally navigable to ships from the North Sea. Thus all trade between northern France, the Low Countries and southern England on the one hand, and Sweden, the Baltic coasts and Russia on the other, passed via Hedeby and Hollingsted. A few miles of overland transport was far preferable to the voyage through the Skagerak and Kattegat, infested with pirates, and round the west coast of Jutland, whose waters were most dangerous to shipping. Hedeby was also well placed for land communications, for it lay on an ancient north–south road linking Jutland and Germany.

Hedeby was already old when Ohthere knew it, probably over 100 years old, though in its early days it had been only a small settlement. In 808 King Godfred of Denmark destroyed a Slavonic town named Reric (possibly near modern Lübeck) and forced its merchants to transfer their activities to Hedeby (at that time called Sliesthorp); in the course of the century it expanded constantly. The site was later fortified by a fine semicircular rampart enclosing some 60 acres, which is thought to date from about 900 when the Swedes were in possession of the town; to the south it was protected by King Godfred's Danevirke. It is not clear how much of this large area was at first built over; possibly a good deal of it was occupied by open-air stalls and by the tents of visiting merchants, peddlars, and ships' crews. But by the middle of the tenth century the actual town had grown considerably, covering graves and settlements of earlier times, and this was

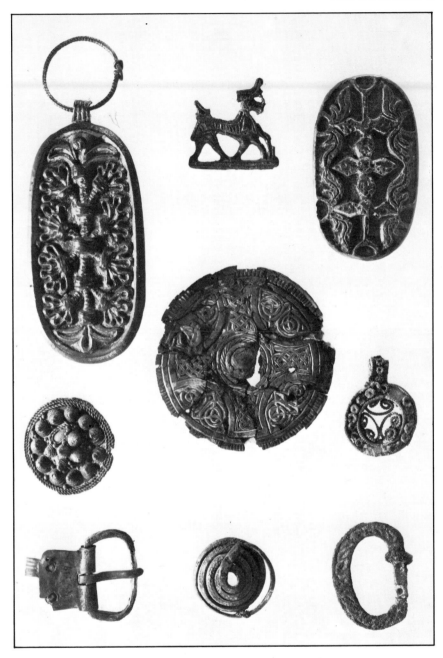

Brooches, pendants etc. found at Hedeby.

the period of Hedeby's greatest prosperity. Gradually it declined, and after it had been burnt by Norwegians in 1050 and sacked by Wends in 1066, its site was abandoned and its role taken over by Sleswig, a little further north.

The oldest dwellings at Hedeby were big timber long-houses, but there soon appeared smaller squarish ones some 10–12 feet each way, which by the tenth century quite ousted the older type. Some of these little houses were built in rows along either side of a well-made wooden road, each separated from it by its own fenced courtyard with path and gateway; others were on the banks of a stream running through the main part of the town, and had steps leading down to the water. Almost all had a well in the yard. In addition there were grave-fields of various periods, with burials totalling several thousands, including a considerable proportion of women and children; evidently there were people who lived at Hedeby with their families all the year round, as well as those who passed through at certain seasons. The types of graves are not all Scandinavian, for there were many Frisians and Saxons there as well.

This permanent population was possible because Hedeby was no mere market, but also a centre for craftsmen, who had quarters of their own. One of its earliest houses (datable to the mid-eighth century by a coin found in it) belonged to a craftsman who left there lumps of raw amber and some half-made beads. Besides amber (both the native Jutland type and that from the Baltic coasts), other raw materials were brought to Hedeby to be worked up – antlers of stags and reindeer, to be made into combs, pins, knife handles, or playing-pieces; walrus tusks; bronze, tin and lead; large quantities of iron-ore, almost all of it good lake-ore from Sweden, not the inferior local type. There were glass-makers, whose ovens show fragments of brightly coloured glass such as was used for beads. There was much metal-working; many broken clay moulds have been found, showing that certain patterns of tortoise brooch were cast here in large numbers, together with an elaborate type of three-lobed brooch, some round brooches, pendants, and figurines. In the tenth century expensive filigree work was produced in silver or occasionally gold, by a complex and delicate technique. Hedeby was probably also the site of the first Scandinavian mint, producing coins intermittently from the early ninth century onwards. Finally, the presence of loom-weights shows that cloth was woven, though it is not known whether this went beyond local needs. Very few agricultural tools have been found; evidently the inhabitants bought their food from elsewhere, though they do seem to have kept pigs.

Various goods came into Hedeby from the south and west, and were imported from there into the rest of Scandinavia: quern stones from round Koblenz, walnuts, big two-handled pottery jars from the Rhineland which probably contained oil or wine, and Frankish glass. It is likely that the Continental sword-blades marked Ulfberht or Inglerii (p.   ) also passed through Hedeby on their way to Norway, and so too the fine cloth found at Kaupang, Birka and elsewhere (p.   ), but in neither case has the trade left traces of its passage.

Not only could the Scandinavians sell the Arctic furs and other wares mentioned already, but they also carried on a flourishing slave trade, part of which passed through Hedeby. The strongest demand for slaves at this period came from the Arabs along the whole Mediterranean coast from Spain to the Middle East; in earlier times this had largely been supplied by the sale of prisoners, debtors and criminals from western and central Europe, but after these regions became Christianized, the Church tried to stamp out the trade – not from any objection to slavery as such, but to prevent Christians having Muslims for their owners. So when the Swedes were able to produce a good supply of undeniably heathen Slavs captured in raids round the Baltic or in Russia, nothing prevented them from passing them through Christian lands in order to sell them to the Arabs. Most of this trade went eastwards down the Russian rivers to the Caspian and Black Sea, but much also went west through Hedeby and passed, by the co-operation of Frankish and Jewish merchants, down the old slave-route to Marseilles, and so the Arabs of Spain and Africa. Thus it came about that the Arab Ibn Khurdadhbih, writing in about 844, lists typically Scandinavian goods as the exports of the Franks to the Muslims: 'eunuchs, male slaves, female slaves, beaver- and marten-skins, and other furs'; while Ibn Hauqal, in 977, refers to Slav eunuchs being sold from Spain to Egypt.

Meanwhile, Danish and Norwegian Vikings were also capturing slaves in their raids on western Europe, especially in Ireland. Since these were Christians they could not be sold in the same way as the others, so they kept them for their own use, chiefly for work on the land. In about 870 Archbishop Rimbert of Hamburg was passing through Hedeby, and felt such pity at the sight of the many Christian slaves there that he spent much of his own money and sold his church vessels to redeem them. On one occasion he saw a whole company passing by, chained together, and guarded by armed men; they cried out that they were Christians, and one told him she was a nun, and sang psalms to prove it, whereupon Rimbert gave his horse to her owners in order to buy her freedom. In all probability these Christian slaves came from the West, and were being taken to be sold to the landowners of southern Norway and Sweden.

It is even possible that the Arabs sometimes came themselves to buy their slaves at Hedeby – at any rate, it is hard to imagine why else an Arab from Cordova, Ibrahim ibn Ahmed at-Tartushi, should have come there in the 950s. He seems to have heartily disliked this 'very large town beyond the furthest end of the ocean', and to have mistakenly interpreted some of its customs as signs of great poverty; nevertheless, his account is interesting:

There are fresh-water wells in the town. Its inhabitants are worshippers of Sirius, except for a few who are Christians and have a church there. They hold a feast at which they all gather to honour their god and to eat and drink. Whoever kills a beast as a sacrifice sets up a pole at the door of his house and hangs the animal up on it (whether ox, ram, he-goat, or pig); thus people know he has made an offering to honour his god. The town is poor in goods and treasure. The main food of the inhabitants is fish, which is very plentiful there. When a child is born, they often throw it into the sea to save expense. Among them, women have the right to claim divorce, and the woman arranges her own divorce whenever she wishes. Also there is an artfully made cosmetic for the eyes; when they use it their beauty does not fade, but on the contrary increases. Never have I heard such hideous singing as that of the people of this town; it is a growl that comes from the throat, like the baying of dogs, only even more like a wild beast than that.

Besides Kaupang and Hedeby, there was a third Scandinavian town at the height of its prosperity towards the close of the ninth century: Birka, on the island of Björkö in Lake Mälar in Sweden. This great lake remained vital to Sweden's commercial life through many centuries; another of its islands, Helgö, had already been a centre for traders and craftsmen from the fifth to the eighth century, and later, in the eleventh, the new town of Sigtuna was built on its shores. The sheltered shallow waters of lakes and estuaries were ideal for the shipping of this period, which drew little water and carried compact cargoes of luxury goods, requiring no elaborate quays and landing-stages for unloading. Small ships could be dragged ashore up a gently shelving beach, large ones moored to posts sunk in shallow water (such as have been found both at Birka and Hedeby), and unloaded by little boats or by men wading out to them. Birka was in fact provided with beaches and coves with water of varying depths, suitable for vessels of every type.

The actual town of Birka covered an area of some 30 acres, most of it so long and intensively inhabited that its soil is still visibly darkened by the accumulation of organic rubbish. Little of this area has so far been excavated, so we cannot yet describe the homes and occupations of the inhabitants as we can at Hedeby. On the other hand, the large groups of graves outside the town have been thoroughly examined, and their contents alone show how wide-ranging were Birka's contacts – glass and pottery from the Rhineland; a very fine woollen fabric, often dyed blue with woad, which may well be the 'Frisian cloth' so much prized in Europe at this period; silks and brocades from Byzantium; finer silks from China; leather belts studded with metal plaques from Persia; little glass gaming-pieces from the Near East; an amethyst ring with an Arabic inscription; and coins, some from western Europe, but many more from the Muslim Caliphates of the East. The native wealth of Scandinavia has also left its traces: amber, walrus tusks, reindeer horn, and fragments of fur of bear, beaver, marten, Arctic fox and otter. Probably it was also from here that iron-ore, such as was found at Hedeby, was exported to the Continent. Copper, too, was mined in Sweden and was used as an inlay on weapons and jewellery.

Birka was protected not merely by its position, so remote from the open sea, but also by a fortified rocky hill a quarter of a mile to the south, 100 feet high, and commanding a good view of all approaches. On one side this hill formed a steep cliff; on the other three it was guarded by earthen ramparts; not far off, deep drifts of ashes in a sheltered hollow overlooking the lake probably mark the spot where beacons were lit to guide ships through the channels from the coast. Later, in the course of the tenth century, the town was enclosed on the landward side by a palisade set on a low stone wall, probably with wooden towers every hundred yards or so.

The earliest references to Birka come in Archbishop Rimbert's *Life of St. Anskar*, written about 870. Anskar was a missionary monk who made great

Glassware from the Rhineland, found at Birka.

Pottery from the Rhineland, found at Birka.

efforts to Christianize the Danes, and lived for some years at Hedeby, from which he set out in about 829 to visit Birka and attempt to convert the Swedes. The journey proved perilous:

> Halfway across they came upon pirates. And although the merchants who were travelling with them defended themselves manfully and were at first victorious, nevertheless in a second onslaught they were beaten and overwhelmed by the pirates, who robbed them of their ship and all they possessed. It was with great difficulty that they got to land and saved their lives. They had to leave behind the kingly gifts [from the Frankish Emperor Louis the Pious] which they had meant to bring to Sweden; they saved only a few petty objects which they could carry with them as they jumped overboard. Among other things they lost almost 40 books which had been meant for the Holy Service, and which fell into the robbers' hands.

Nevertheless, Anskar was well received by King Bjorn at Birka, was allowed to build a church there, and remained for two years till recalled to become Archbishop of Hamburg.

In about 850 Anskar revisited Birka, and the narrative again reveals what a serious problem piracy was at this period. In the course of an Assembly where the Swedes were debating religious matters, one of the merchants of Birka reminded them of their past journeys to Dorestad, the great Frisian trading-centre at the mouth of the Rhine, where many of them had been willing to accept Christianity; but 'nowadays there are many obstacles to be feared before one reaches Dorestad, and because of pirate attacks the way has become most dangerous to us'. This may well allude to the repeated raids of Danish Vikings on this town from 834 onwards.

The *Life of St. Anskar* is naturally mainly concerned with these links between Birka and the Christian West, but in fact its most important traffic was with the East, by the long trade-routes which the Swedes had opened up along the rivers of Russia. It was a good centre for exporting the furs hunted in northern Sweden; moreover, successful merchants returning from the East brought with them hundreds of silver coins, and the market of Birka was certainly one of the main places at which this money was spent and dispersed through the rest of Sweden.

The eastern route lay along the Gulf of Finland, and so up the Neva to the areas of north Russia round Lake Ladoga. At this period these regions were inhabited by Finnish-speaking peoples, so that communication was easy for the Swedes, who had already had many occasions of contact with Finns during their ninth-century expansion round the eastern Baltic (p. 21). The very name *Rus* is in all probability a corruption of *Ruotsi*, the Finnish word for 'Swedes', later adopted by Slavs, Muslims and Byzantines as a name for Swedish traders in Russia, or for the men of the mixed Swedish and Slavonic communities that established themselves along the Dnieper.

A few miles south of Lake Ladoga, near the present town of Staraya Ladoga, stood a town which had been founded by Finns, but which shows many signs of Swedish habitation in the ninth and tenth centuries; the graves of this region often contain ornaments and other objects from Sweden, but it is a matter of dispute whether this proves that they were actually graves of Swedes, or merely those of Finns who had traded with Swedes. If the first is true, one must envisage the Ladoga area as one of large-scale settlement and colonization, in which Swedes lived side by side with Finns, forming an agricultural community in which the two races were gradually assimilated to each other.

Be this as it may, there is no doubt of Ladoga's importance as the starting-point for trade-routes that went by water. By going north-east up the Svir one reached Lake Onega, and from there the regions round the White Sea, rich hunting-grounds for skin-traders. But the main route ran south, up the river Volkhov to Lake Ilmen and the stronghold of Novgorod (called Holmgard by Scandinavians), whose population was mainly Slav, but ruled by a Scandinavian dynasty. Leaving Lake Ilmen, one would row south up the river Lovat and one or other of its many tributaries, drag the boats overland across the watershed, and launch them again at the source of either of two mighty rivers – the Dnieper, leading to the Black Sea and so to Byzantium, or the Volga, leading to the Caspian and the caravan routes of the East. These were the highways along which the Scandinavian merchants plied their trade.

Map of Viking Age trade-routes.

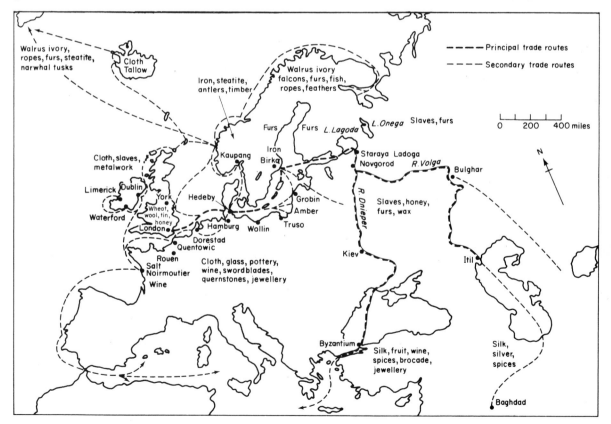

Swedish activities in Russia must have begun early in the ninth century. The Frankish *Annals of St. Bertin* record that in 839 Byzantine ambassadors visiting the Emperor Louis the Pious had in their train some men of Swedish origin, calling themselves *Rhos*; they had been sent by their ruler in northern Russia to Byzantium (presumably down the Dnieper), but could not go back the same way because the route was overrun by fierce barbarian tribes, and so they were having to make their way home by this huge detour through France.

The *Annals* do not say that these *Rhos* were merchants, but the Arab Ibn Khurdadhbih explicitly speaks of the Rus as traders; he calls them 'a sort of *as-Saqaliba*' (a name applied to Slavs and to various neighbouring peoples), but despite this confusion he almost certainly means the Swedes. He tells how they travel by river, 'bringing beaver-skins, and skins of black foxes, and swords, from the furthest parts of the Slav lands down to the Black Sea', and paying toll to the Greek Emperor on their wares; or else they follow the *Tana' is* (either the Don or the upper Volga), pass through a Khazar town on the Volga (paying tolls there too), and reach the Caspian, which they cross by ship, and sometimes bring their wares by camel as far as to Baghdad. Thus it seems from this circumstantial account that the two great trade-routes were both in regular use before the middle of the ninth century.

In the course of time fortified towns sprang up along the Dnieper at Smolensk, Chernigov and Kiev; these were ruled by warrior aristocracies of Scandinavian descent, though whether the bulk of the inhabitants were Slav or Scandinavian is still in dispute. Relationships between the two races were certainly complex: on the one hand, the Scandinavians exacted tribute from the Slavs, and carried many of them off as slaves, but at the same time they themselves became increasingly Slavicized in customs and by inter-marriage.

The way of life of these merchants of the Dnieper valley is well described by the Byzantine Emperor Constantine Porphyrogenitus, writing in about 950:

> In winter the life of the Rus is hard. At the beginning of November the chieftains and all the Rus leave Kiev together and go to their round forts [or: 'go on their rounds'; the text is obscure] in the regions of . . . the Slav tribes who owe tribute to the Rus. There they remain all winter, but in the month of April, when the ice of the Dnieper has melted, they come back to Kiev.

For their river journeys, the Scandinavians did not use their own finely built craft, but smaller and cruder boats made locally. The Emperor continues:

> At Kiev they destroy their old dug-out canoes and buy fresh ones from the Slavs, who have been hewing them out during the winter in their forests. They take the baling-scoops, thwarts and other gear out of the old boats and fit out the new ones with these. In June the expedition sets out

for Greece. For a few days the merchant fleet assembles at Vytechev, a fortress of the Rus just below Kiev. When the fleet is complete they all set off downstream, so as to face the difficulties of the journey in company.

The chief of these difficulties is a series of fierce cataracts and rapids where the Dnieper forces its way through granite gorges near Dnjepropetrovsk. The Emperor describes seven of these, giving them both Scandinavian and Slavonic names; some, for instance the first, are not too dangerous:

> In the middle of it there are high sheer rocks, which look like islands; when the water reaches them and dashes against them it causes a loud and terrifying tumult as it crashes down. Therefore the Rus do not dare sail between them, but lay their boats alongside the bank before this point and make the people go up on shore, though they leave the cargo on board. Then they walk into the water naked, testing the bottom with their feet so as not to stumble over stones; at the same time they thrust the boat forwards with poles, many of them at the bows, many amidships, and others at the stern. With all these precautions they wade through the edge of these first rapids, close along the bank; as soon as they have passed them, they take the rest of the crew back on board, and go on their way by boat.

But others need more elaborate measures:

> At the fourth great rapids . . . they all put into the bank with their vessel, and the men whose task it is to keep guard disembark. These guards are necessary because of the Patzinaks, who are always lurking in ambush. The rest of them take their goods out of the canoes and lead their slaves, fettered in chains, for six miles over dry land, till they have passed beyond the rapids. After this they transport their boats past the rapids, partly dragging them, partly carrying them on their shoulders, and then put them back on the river, load their baggage in, get in themselves, and go on their way.

When all the rapids have been safely passed, they pause for a rest, and to make a thank-offering:

> Then they succeed in reaching an island, named after St Gregory, to which they bring their offerings because a gigantic oak-tree grows there. They make offerings of live birds; they stick javelins in a circle in the ground round them; others make offerings of bread and meat too, and of whatever they each may have, as is the prevailing custom among them. Also they cast lots over the birds, whether they should slaughter them, or eat them themselves, or let them free.

So they came at length to the mouth of the Dnieper and the island Berezanj, where in 1905 archaeologists found a rune-stone raised by a Gotlander named Grani as a memorial to his comrade Karl. From there, they follow

Viking merchants carrying boats overland in Russia (Olaus Magnus, 1555).

the Black Sea coast to Byzantium.

To judge from the great numbers of Arabic and Persian coins found in Sweden and north Russia, there was far more trading by the Volga route than with Byzantium. Two Khaganates (independent empires) existed on the Volga; that of the Bulghars, originally Turkish nomads, who had settled round the great bend of the Volga, where their town named Bulghar was an important trading-centre; and that of the Khazars who were established on the southern reaches of the Volga with their capital at Itil, where it flows into the Caspian. All the trade of the Volga was controlled by these two peoples; they had close contact with the Caliphate of Baghdad, and were often visited by Arab merchants from the south and east. It was these Arabs to whom the Scandinavians sold their slaves and northern produce for silver, and from whom they also probably sometimes took silk and spices in exchange.

Several tenth-century Muslim writers allude to these Rus traders, and two describe them in some detail. One, the geographer Ibn Rustah, says of them:

> As for the Rus, they live on an island in a lake [Novgorod on Lake Ilmen?]. The island they live on takes three days to walk round and is covered with thick undergrowth and forests; it is most unhealthy and so marshy that the ground yields underfoot. They have a prince called Hagan-Rus. They harry the Slavs, using ships to reach them; they carry them off as captives and take them to Hazaran and Bulghar [both on the Volga], and sell them there. They have no fields, but simply live on what they get from the Slavs' lands. . . . They have no domains, settlements or fields; their only business is to trade in sable and squirrel skins and other kinds of skin, selling them to those who will buy from them. In payment they take coins, which they keep in their belts.

A merchant's scales and rings.

Head of a Viking: detail from the Oseberg wagon.

The evidence of the other Arab, Ibn Fadlan, is even more valuable, for he based his detailed and lengthy account of the appearance, customs and beliefs of the Rus on what he himself saw of them when he went on a diplomatic mission from Baghdad to Bulghar in 922. At certain seasons, he says, they gather there for the markets:

They arrive from their own lands and moor their ships along the Itil [Volga], which is a great river, and build large wooden houses on its banks. In one such house 10 or 20 people (or more, or less) will gather. Each of them has a bench on which he sits, and beside him sits one of the lovely girls destined for sale to merchants, and he will make love with his girl while his comrades look on. It may often happen that they are all at this, openly, in one another's sight, and that a merchant comes in to buy a girl from one of them, and so comes upon him while he is making love with her, but the other will not let her go till he has had all he wants. . . .

When their ships arrive at their anchorage, each man goes on shore taking with him bread, meat, leeks, milk and beer, and goes to a tall upright wooden post with a face that looks like a man's. Round it there are smaller figures, and behind these figures high wooden poles planted in the ground. So he goes up to the big figure, flings himself on the ground, and says: 'O my Lord, I have come from far off with so many girls and so many sable skins' (here he counts up all the wares he has brought), 'and now I come to you with this offering.' (Thereupon he lays what he has brought in front of the wooden post.) 'I pray that you should send me a merchant who has many dinars and dirhems, who will buy from me as I wish, and will not contradict what I say.' So he goes away. And if his trade meets with difficulties and time is being wasted, he returns with one or two more offerings. If he still finds difficulties, he brings an offering to each of the small figures and begs their intercession, saying: 'These are the wives and daughters and sons of our Lord.' Thus he goes from one figure to another, praying to them and hoping they will intercede for him, and humbling himself before them. But often his trade goes easily, so that he makes his sale straight away; in that case he says: 'My Lord has seen to my needs; now it is my duty to repay him.' So he goes to fetch a number of sheep and cattle, and slaughters them. Some of the flesh he gives as alms; the rest he takes and throws between the big post and the smaller ones surrounding it; the heads of the cattle and sheep he hangs up on the poles planted in the earth. After dark the dogs come and eat all this up; the man who has done it says: 'Clearly, my Lord is pleased with me and has eaten my offerings.'

Ibn Fadlan also describes the wives of these Rus merchants, whose attire sounds very like that described in Chapter 3:

Each of their wives has a container on each breast [the tortoise brooch?]; it is firmly fastened on, and is of iron, silver, copper or gold, according to the amount and value of her husband's wealth. On each container there is a ring, from which hangs a knife, also fastened firmly to her breast. Round their necks the women wear neck-rings of gold or silver; when a man has 10,000 dirhems, he gives his wife a neck-ring; when he has 20,000 he gives two rings, and in this way the wife gets a neck-ring for every 10,000 dirhems that the man adds to his wealth. Often one woman has many rings round her neck. Ornaments much valued among them are beads of green glass; they go to much trouble to get these, paying one dirhem for a bead, and stringing them into necklaces for their wives.

Of the men, Ibn Fadlan says that they are handsome and as tall as date-palms, but repulsively dirty in their personal habits; their ruler lives in a fort, with a bodyguard of 400 warriors and harem of 40 slavegirls. He also gives a long description of their funeral rites, which will be discussed in Chapter 9. The accounts of these Muslim writers are tinged with the amused curiosity of men of an advanced civilization confronted with those they regard as barbarians, but on the whole they seem to present a reliable picture of the Scandinavian merchants plying their trade in Russia.

The wealth won in the East flowed back into Sweden in the form of silver; some 85,000 Arabic and about 500 Byzantine coins have been found so far in various parts of Scandinavia, almost all of them dating from the ninth and tenth centuries. Towards the close of this period the silver mines of the Baghdad Caliphate became exhausted, and in the ensuing economic upheavals Swedish trade with the Arabs came to an end. Instead, the Scandinavians increased their trade with Germany, where the silver of the Harz mountains was beginning to be exploited; about 70,000 German coins have been found in Scandinavia, dating from the later tenth and the eleventh centuries. At the same period thousands of English coins appeared, but these do not represent the profits of trade so much as the Danegelds exacted by the raiders and the pay earned by warriors in the service of Svein and Cnut.

Native Scandinavian coinage first appears early in the ninth century, and is thought to have been minted at Hedeby; production seems to have been spasmodic, and on a moderate scale only. In the British Isles, however, numerous coins were issued during the tenth century by Scandinavian kings in York and other Danelaw towns, and in Dublin, at the end of that century, the first truly national coinages appear in Denmark, Norway and Sweden.

Coins, however, were not treated as true currency but simply reckoned by weight; many are found cut in halves or quarters for the payment of small sums, and hoarded up side by side with 'hacksilver' (that is, silver rings and ornaments chopped up into arbitrary pieces), and with bars cast to obtain definite weights. Silver circulated equally freely in all these forms, broken up or melted down as was convenient; hacksilver in particular had long been an established medium of payment.

Naturally, scales and weights were indispensable, and many have been found in graves; not only would far-travelling merchants need them, but at home the hunters, craftsmen and farmers must have used them when they sold their produce to passing traders or visited the local markets, for Scandinavian economy certainly no longer functioned simply by barter and payments in kind. Particularly attractive among the scales are the delicate collapsible bronze ones, made probably in Ireland, and very popular in Norway; over 40 sets have been found there, often carefully packed in a box or pouch, or in their original spherical bronze or copper cases. One set from Sigtuna in Sweden has a runic inscription on the case, recording that its owner got it from a man in Samland (an area of East Prussia, rich in amber), and adding two lines of verse, apparently a boast of how the owner killed a thief and left his body for the crows:

> *A bird ripped up the robber pale,*
> *I saw the carrion-cuckoo swell.*

The scale-pans are only two or three inches across, for the units of weight were not large. One widespread system was based on three units, the *ertog* of 8·67 grams, the *øre* of 24·55 grams (roughly one ounce), and the *mark* of 204 grams. Actual weights found at Hedeby correspond closely to the theoretical *ertog* and *øre*, and others include several 'double-*øre*' averaging 49·5 grams, and two 'half-*marks*' of about 100 grams. Such weights were made of lead or iron. In two ninth-century hoards not far from Hedeby there are specimens of silver prepared to fit this system – three rings and one bar weighing one

Sledge from Oseberg ship

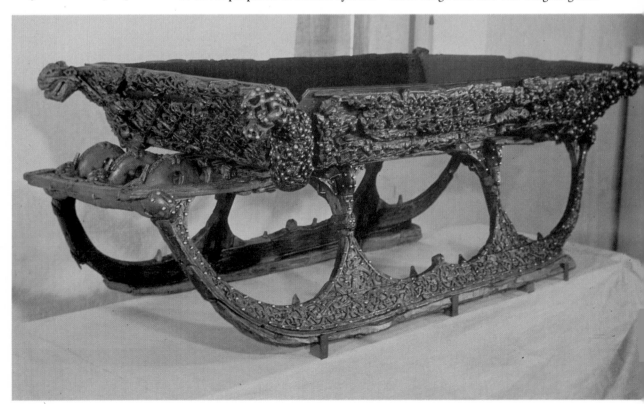

øre each, 14 bars of the 'double-*øre*' weight, and two of the 'half-*mark*'. Evidently when a man's purse became too full of small coin fragments and clippings from thin rings, he would have them melted down and cast into these neat bars corresponding to the standard weights. Dishonest people, it may be added, occasionally passed off bars with a mere coating of silver round an iron core.

It is likely that merchants kept written records of their transactions in the form of wooden tablets inscribed in runic writing. Over 500 tablets were recently excavated in Bergen (Norway), and a high proportion of them were tally-sticks, records of ownership, and similar commercial documents. Although they are of post-Viking date, i.e. of the twelfth and thirteenth centuries, one can plausibly assume that similar tablets were used earlier, for literacy was quite normal in the Viking Age (see below, p. 149); one can hope that earlier examples will be found on sites where conditions permit the survival of wood.

Long-distance trade always went by water, whether by sea or along river-systems; however, there was also local trade that must have gone by land. Many widespread native articles, for instance certain types of brooch or arm-ring, show such strong similarities that they must have been mass-produced in certain centres and sold at local markets. It is also likely that craftsmen and small traders moved about the country – such as the owner of one well-stocked tool-chest found in Gotland, who was evidently both smith

A blacksmith's tools with swordblades and axeheads, from Norway.

and carpenter, mender of cauldrons, and maker of locks and cowbells which he carried round for sale. Nor must one forget that market-towns also served the needs of local trade, just as much as of the long-distance trade described above; craft products were for home consumption as well as for export.

Winter was in some ways the best time for travelling, for rivers and swamps were frozen solid, and hill slopes smooth with snow. Skis and snow-shoes were much used; there were also bone skates cut to fit the foot, which one used by thrusting oneself over the ice with a spiked stick, hardly lifting one's feet. Many such skates were found at Birka, and also ice-crampons fitted to men's shoes. Clearly, the activities of Birka were not halted by winter – indeed, when the lake and its approaches were frozen it would make an excellent site for a winter market, at the very season when furs were at their best.

In winter, goods could be transported on sledges, of which several have been found in graves where the soil allowed the preservation of wood; in others, only the heavy hooks by which they were hitched up have been preserved. Normally they were drawn by two horses, their shoes fitted with crampons. The bodywork of the sledge was only loosely attached to the runners; at Oseberg, some were interchangeable, while another did not fit the runners it was found with. It has been suggested that the same bodies could be fitted to a wheeled frame for summer and to runners for winter, and perhaps even be lifted into boats if the journey was partly by water.

In summer, the chief means of transport was the horse, for riding, as a pack animal, and for drawing wagons. Much harness and riding gear has been found in Viking Age graves, some of it ordinary everyday equipment, some the lavish gear of chieftains. There are also many representations of riders in the art of the period. The horses were certainly smaller than modern ones, and seem to have had thicker necks and shorter backs; the Oseberg Tapestry and a sketch of a horse's hindquarters on a broken slate from Jarlshof show tails tied in an ornamental knot, though elsewhere they are plain. One curious item often found among harness in Norway is a rattle of iron rings; one type was set on a shaft, while the other was fitted with hooks, suggesting that it dangled from the harness or from the mane itself. Small bells are sometimes found with these; both bells and rattles might well be charms to scare off evil spirits.

Although the only wagon surviving from the Viking Age, that from Oseberg, must from the lavishness of its carvings have been a ceremonial carriage, there is no reason to doubt that there were also wagons and carts for practical use, however rough the tracks must often have been in summer. One section of the Oseberg Tapestry shows what appear to be horse-drawn baggage-wagons, their piled-up contents covered by cloths – or possibly the whole thing is meant to be tented over like an American prairie-wagon. Two are led by men walking beside them, the other driven by one of two figures riding in it; all are accompanied by spearmen and other figures on foot. The scene is very likely part of some myth or legend, yet similar convoys may well have been a familiar sight on the roads of Scandinavia.

Ornate horse-collars, from
Denmark.

The best evidence concerning Viking roads comes from Sweden in the eleventh century, though that is not to say that they were lacking in other regions and earlier times. Indeed, Snorri Sturluson attributes the first Swedish roads to a very early king named Onund, who, he says, had tracks cleared through forests and swamps and over mountains. This may be mere legend, but it certainly was the custom later for kings to travel through their domains; roads would also have been needed leading to major temples and Assembly-places, as well as to trading-centres. The earliest must have been natural tracks, for instance those running along the smooth, grassy mountain ridges of Sweden, which needed little improvement beyond

A loaded wagon: detail from the Oseberg Tapestry.

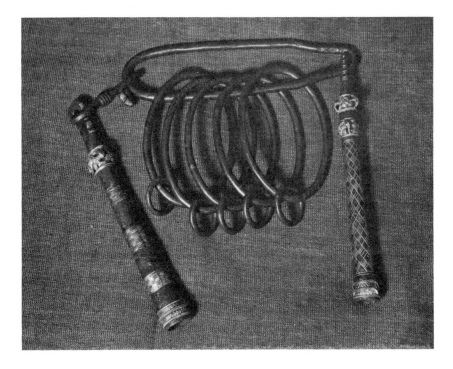

A horseman's rattle, found in the Oseberg ship.

laying stone slabs to give a firmer footing at some fords; but valley roads, which had to pass through woods and over marshy and clayey soil, needed constant careful upkeep.

It had long been a Scandinavian custom to raise stones in memory of the dead, preferably by the roadside or near a ford, where they would be seen by all the passers-by. From about 1000 onwards large numbers of such stones were raised in Sweden (and a few elsewhere), with inscriptions that not merely commemorate the dead but add that some relative 'made this bridge' in his honour and for the good of his soul – 'bridge' in these cases meaning any sort of structure to make the road more passable, such as a causeway over marshes, a better ford, and of course actual wooden bridges too.

These stones were raised by Christians, as the phrasing clearly shows in many cases, and it is likely that the practice of road-making was encouraged by the Church, which considered it a useful charity; there are many instances from other parts of Europe later in the Middle Ages where the Church granted indulgences for the living and dead to those who improved bridges and roads. One Norwegian stone is carved with pictures of the Three Magi journeying to Bethlehem, a very suitable subject for a work done in charity to travellers; its inscription reads: 'Gunnvor, Thidrik's daughter, made this bridge in memory of her daughter Astrid; she was the most skilful maiden in Hadeland'.

The works involved were often extensive. At Läby, near Uppsala, one can still trace more than 300 yards of causeway crossing swampy ground, quite wide enough for wagons; the basis is a layer of gravel one foot deep and 20 feet wide, over which comes a layer of large stone blocks some 15 feet wide, then a bed of brushwood, and probably a final covering of gravel; at one point the structure is interrupted by a river, which must have been spanned by a wooden bridge. At one end of the causeway stand two rune-stones, saying: 'Jarl and Karl and Jokulbjorn had these stones raised and this bridge made in memory of their father Jofur. God help his soul.'

Traces of many such causeways remain, and there were also true bridges. For instance, the Ramsund Rock, famous for its picture of the Sigurd Legend, marks the spot where a woman named Sigrid commemorated her husband by a wooden bridge some 200 feet long crossing water about 10 feet deep, together with a causeway leading to it. Sometimes the occurrence of several stones near the same spot shows that a bridge or causeway needed rebuilding at intervals, often by kinsmen of the first builder. Most of these stones stand in their places to the present day, with the modern road still following its old course beside them; not surprisingly, the pride of those who raised such memorials rings out in their inscriptions, most notably in that of the Sälna Stone – unfortunately slightly damaged:

Eystein and Jorund and Bjorn, brothers, raised [this stone in memory of X] their father. God help his soul and spirit, and forgive him his offences and sins.

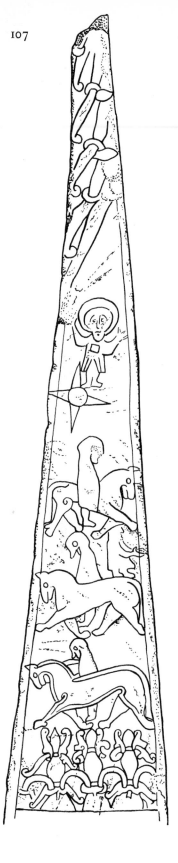

Astrid's memorial stone.

While the world lasts,
Ever will lie
This bridge, a good man's,
Broad, firm-based.
To a father's honour
Youths fashioned this.
Nobler sign by the roadside
There never shall be.

In Denmark, the chief road was the famous Haervej, 'Army Way', which passed by Hedeby (see above, p. 88); it was ancient in origin, dating from Roman times, and its upkeep through centuries of constant use must have given the Danes valuable experience in road-making. One branch of it passes by the royal centre of Jelling, near which a remarkable wooden bridge about threequarters of a mile long crossed a marshy valley. It is built on wooden piles, each exactly one foot square, and each set at precisely the same distance from its neighbour in four parallel rows, the outer ones being strengthened by raking piles which helped to support the actual trackway. The latter has nowhere survived, but the strength of the piles shows that it could have carried weights up to five tons. This remarkable structure can be precisely dated by dendrochronology to within one or two years of 979, in the reign of Harald Bluetooth; it may have remained in use for about a century, but was apparently never repaired. Beyond it lay a stretch of road which has recently been excavated, and which shows signs of careful planning, for instance in the way steep slopes are reduced by hollowing the surface, and the way that cobbled strips are laid to take cartwheels but the central area is left uncobbled to spare the hoofs of horses and oxen.

Clearly, there is no need to take as typical the unlucky experiences of the poet Sighvat Thordsson, who bemoans the discomforts of a journey from Norway to Sweden in the winter of 1018 – his sore feet, the weariness of crossing leagues of forest, the ramshackle ferryboat, the inhospitable farmers. On the contrary, land communications were fairly good, by medieval standards, and if the sagas more often mention journeys to courts and Assemblies than to markets, this is simply due to the chosen subject matter of these sources. In the Viking Age, aptly called the Silver Age of Scandinavia, there were ample opportunities for wealth to circulate both by external and internal trade, and both by land and water.

6
Weapons and Warriors

Though there was no such thing as a purely warrior caste in Scandinavia, every Norseman of the Viking Age had to be, to some extent, a fighting man. Those who were farmers at home might at any time join the roving bands of raiders for a few months or years, or might set out to find themselves new land – not always peacefully. The merchants travelled far and wide, and must always be prepared to defend their goods against robbers on land and pirates at sea. Even in a settled community with no external enemies, such as the Icelandic sagas show us, the risk of feuds was always close at hand. In death the heathen Viking took weapons to the grave, and in life they were rarely far from his side by night or day:

Spearman in boar-crested helmet; seventh century.

> In the fields no man should stir one step
> From where his weapons are,
> For it's hard to tell when he'll need a spear
> As he walks out on his way.

The Vikings fought on foot. They naturally used horses to deploy their raiding-bands swiftly, and in their art they often showed mounted warriors, but all descriptions of warfare make it clear that those who rode to the battlefield dismounted there, tethering their horses before the fighting began. This was also the custom among the Anglo-Saxons, as the poem *The Battle of Maldon* describes; similarly, in the battle-scenes on the Gotland stones the horses are shown riderless, either held or tethered. Archaeology confirms this; the horses laid in Viking graves may have rich harness, stirrups and other trappings near them, but never a trace of any horse-armour, such as would surely have been invented if it had been the custom to use steeds in battle.

In the earliest period the chief weapons were the sword and spear; later, the axe often replaced the spear, and came to be regarded as the typical weapon of the Vikings. They also used the *sax*, a species of long knife or one-edged sword, and sometimes also a bow and arrows. Shields were round and fairly small. The corselet or mail-shirt of interlinked iron rings is often mentioned in literature, but only rarely have small fragments of such mail been found; probably corselets were fairly short, unlike the long ones shown on the Bayeux Tapestry. The majority of fighting men could not afford mail, and relied instead on padded leather jerkins, bone plaques sewn inside their clothing, and similar home-made protections. Even leaders sometimes chose to wear such jerkins; it is said that one of the nobles in revolt against St Olaf had 12 coats of reindeer hide made by Lapps for himself and his closest followers, and that these could turn a blow as well as any mail-coat.

Swedish and Danish laws of the twelfth century state that every able-bodied man should own, besides weapons, an 'iron hat'; yet, oddly enough, helmets of the Viking Age are even rarer and more fragmentary than corselets. Pictures and carvings show them as small conical caps (whether metal or leather is hard to tell), and towards the end of the period they sometimes had the straight nose-piece so well known from the Bayeux Tapestry. On the Gotland stones one also sees warriors wearing small round caps that fit closely to the contours of the head, and occasionally some whose helmets are crowned with a spike – a Slav fashion sometimes adopted by Swedes in Russia. These helmets are all plain and functional, and unadorned with the horns and wings so often shown in modern illustrations.

Yet in earlier centuries helmets had been far more ornate, at least among kingly families such as those whose graves lay at Vendel and Valsgärde in Sweden. There, helmets from the late seventh century cover the whole head and face with cheek- and neck-guards, and are enriched with much decoration, including eyebrow ridges which give them the aspect of a

A seventh-century helmet from Vendel.

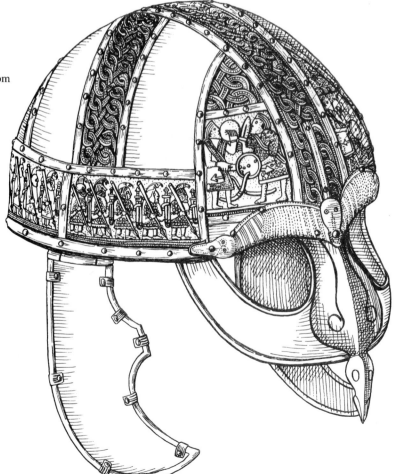

fearsome mask; the well-known helmet from the Anglo-Saxon mound at Sutton Hoo is the same type, and certainly comes from Sweden. It may be that these elaborate helmets were still being produced in Viking times, at least in some areas, for a pair of the characteristic eyebrow ridges were found in Gotland, inlaid with silver and copper in a pattern of Viking style. There is also a tenth-century helmet shaped like a spiked cap with a metal brim and a heavy nose- and eye-guard which is a development from the Vendel helmets. But, even if they were still sometimes made for kings or wealthy chieftains, they were certainly no part of the ordinary man's equipment.

No actual helmet from the Vendel or the Viking period has horns on it. Indirectly, however, there is some evidence that such may once have existed, for the rich Vendel helmets were decorated with embossed plaques showing human figures, and some of these themselves wear helmets with huge crests shaped like boars or birds of prey, or with crescent horns sweeping up from the sides. In general, the weapons shown on these plaques (and on the dies for making them) accurately represent types really used in seventh-century Scandinavia; it is therefore quite possible that horned helmets existed too, but it does not follow that they were common objects, or meant for daily use. The plaques in question were almost certainly designed for magical protection as well as ornament, so that figures on them are unlikely to be ordinary warriors; more probably they represent deities of war, or initiates performing a religious ritual (pp. 138–9, 145).

From the Viking Age itself we have three representations of men in horned helmets: a metal figurine from Birka, another from Ekhammar (Uppland, Sweden), and the Oseberg Tapestry. They are very similar, and clearly descended from the figures on the seventh-century plaques; scenes on the Oseberg Tapestry are probably drawn from myth or legend, and the two figurines may well be amulets. All in all, therefore, it seems best to assume that horned helmets had always been rare, and that in the Viking Age they were remembered only as symbols of religious power.

Probably the most widespread weapon was the spear, of which many different types have been found, varying in the size or shape of the spear-head, according as they were designed for casting or for thrusting. The names applied to spears are also very various; some are identical with those applied to arrows, and probably refer to very light darts for casting. Some were called 'twisting spears', and are said to have been thrown with a cord looped about their shaft, so that they spun in flight; weapons of this type go back to the Migration Age and have been found in the bogs of Denmark, their cords still twisted round them. Other spear-shafts from these ancient bogs have studs or bindings set at the centre of gravity, to show where they should be gripped for a good cast; this was probably also the case with Viking spears (cf. the broken spears of the duellists on the brow of the helmet on p. 110, which seem to show grips of the same sort).

Skill in casting spears was greatly valued, and must have been constantly practised. Some men could cast two at once, one from each hand; this was one of the most famous feats of King Olaf Tryggvason. Many years after

Silver amulet of a man in a horned helmet.

Olaf's death a man calling himself Tryggvi, and claiming to be a son of Olaf's by a foreign marriage, tried to win the throne of Norway; his rivals mockingly declared that he was only a priest's son, but in his last battle Tryggvi stood flinging spears from both hands at once and crying: '*That* was how my father taught me to say Mass!'

Another skilled feat often described in sagas was to catch a spear in mid-air and fling it back at the enemy without a pause; this was done by dodging to one side, catching the passing spear with a back-handed movement, and swinging one's arm round in a backward circle so that the spear was brought round and up again all in one movement, and was pointing the right way for the return cast.

When the casting weapons were exhausted the fighters would close in for

Spearheads with ornamented sockets.

hand-to-hand fighting, in which thrusting-spears were often used. These have broader, heavier heads, sometimes with long sockets so that they should not be hacked away from the shaft; they are more likely than the casting-spears to be enriched with silver inlay, for there was far less risk of losing them in battle. Yet the thrusting-spear may well have been a later invention than the casting-spear, for in the conservative language of poetry references to spears always allude to their flight.

Another weapon that developed comparatively late was the battleaxe, which evolved by progressive increases of size and weight from earlier axes chiefly used as tools. There were three main types. The 'hand-axe' still had many features of a tool: its head was fairly light, with a useful hammer opposite the blade, and it was set on a long iron-shod shaft; it was very much the farmer's weapon, and men might carry it about in daily life, partly as tool and walking-stick, and partly in case of a surprise attack. The 'bearded axe' was so called because of its characteristic square-cut projection on the lower edge of the blade; it was particularly favoured in sea battles, for its shape was useful in grappling and boarding. The third and best-known type was the famous 'broad-axe', a heavy, long-handled weapon which needed two hands to wield it; its flaring blade might measure as much as 12 inches across, and might be inlaid with silver, gold or niello. The axe became a favourite weapon of the Vikings, who seem to have regarded it with humorous affection and familiarity, contrasting with the awe and mystique surrounding the sword; such at least is the impression given by poetic vocabulary, where terms applied to axes are drawn from the grotesque world of ogresses rather than from lofty myths and legends. 'Swords,' says Snorri, 'are named "fires of Odin", but men call axes by the names of she-trolls and take images for them from blood or wounds or forests or timber.'

Of all Scandinavian weapons, the sword can be studied in the fullest detail, not simply because so many examples have survived but because so many passages in poetry and prose describe the sword's appearance or its making or the use of it in fighting. In earlier times swords had probably been exclusive to men of rank and wealth, and even in the Viking Age, when the use of them had become far more widespread, a certain glamour always clung to them. Good blades were heirlooms, often with names of their own, and sometimes surrounded with legends and taboos; the sword was the symbol of the king's or chieftain's authority, on which oaths of allegiance were sworn; a sword was a fitting gift with which to reward a loyal warrior or a poet, and, like ships, a never-failing subject for poetic ingenuity.

The first essential for a sword was that its blade should not bend, for fighting was a matter of heavy sweeping strokes with the edge, not of thrusting with the point. To obtain the necessary strength one had to increase the natural carbon content of the available iron ores, which was too low; at first, this was done by the elaborate and beautiful technique known as pattern-welding, which had been known long before the Viking Age. A pattern-welded blade was built up out of many thin bars of case-hardened iron – that is, iron that had been packed in charcoal and kept red-hot until its surfaces had absorbed enough carbon to turn them into steel, though the core of the bar was still iron. The bars would be dark at the core, but paler on their steely surfaces. Then, in order to distribute the steely parts more evenly, the bars would be several times cut up and reforged twisted together in a different order; eventually a group of such twisted bars would be welded together to form the central portion of the blade. On to this would be welded two strips of the finest steel to form the cutting edges. The whole blade would then be ground and filed into shape, and during this process a pattern would emerge along the central section, where the intertwined strips of steely and plain iron would show up in patterns of light and dark like eddying waves, coiling snakes, twigs, or sheaves of corn. The aim of the welding was purely functional, but the resulting patterns so struck the imaginations of the Germanic peoples that allusions to them became part of stock poetic vocabulary both in Scandinavia and among the Anglo-Saxons. In particular, the apt comparison of a sword to a deadly snake continued in use long after pattern-welding was no longer practised.

If the carbon content of a blade was high enough, it could be made still harder by 'quenching' it; for this, the blade would be heated once again, and then cooled as fast and violently as possible, by plunging it into some liquid. It is not known what liquid was used; probably not plain water, which all too easily forms a barrier of steam around the blade and so prevents the rapid loss of heat. Oil, honey or wet clay have all been suggested as possibilities; the process seems to have been a closely guarded secret of the swordsmiths. Not surprisingly, one finds occasional traces of a belief that swords might be quenched in blood and would then be more than ordinarily effective. In *Beowulf* one especially noble sword is said to be 'hardened in blood'; in one episode of *Njal's Saga* a man tells how he met Njal's son-in-law Kari after he escaped from the fire in which the rest of the family died, and how he was carrying his sword – 'one of its edges was blue and discoloured, and we said that the metal must have gone soft, but Kari answered that he would soon harden it again in the blood of Sigfus's sons and the others who had done the burning'.

Finally, the blade would have its edges filed and its whole surface made smooth and gleaming by rubbing it with some mild acid such as vinegar, urine, or tannic acid, which would also tend to bring out the pattern even more clearly. This acid treatment may be the reason why poets sometimes speak of 'poison' in connection with weapons, for it is not thought at all likely that they were literally poisoned. One Eddic poem describes the sword of Sigurd the Volsung in a way which seems to refer to the processes of its making:

> *By fire were its outer edges forged,*
> *By venom drops was it tinged within.*

Pattern-welding was already an ancient technique by the time of the Vikings, and towards the end of the ninth century it was replaced (at least in the West, though possibly not among the Swedes in Russia) by blades of a

Forging Sigurd's sword. Helped by Regin, he forges a sword; kills the dragon; roasts its heart and tastes its blood on his thumb; loads the dragon's gold on his horse; and kills Regin. The topmost scene shows another hero, Gunnar, playing a harp in a snake-pit. These carvings are panels from the doors of a church at Hylestad, Norway.

new type. These have a much higher carbon content, which can be as high as 75 per cent, and the carbon is uniformly distributed throughout, so that pattern-welding is no longer needed; this change must have arisen from a major improvement in the quality of ores available, and perhaps also in the construction of furnaces. The new blades are not only tougher but lighter and more shapely; they taper sharply, and their centre of gravity is closer to the hilt, which makes them easier to wield in rapid strokes.

The finest blades of this new type are inlaid with the name 'Ulfberht'; they first appear a little before 900, and continued to be made for over 200 years, presumably by a group of descendants and apprentices of the original Ulfberht, whose name they kept in use as a trade-mark, cleverly worked into the blade and not easily to be forged. From the distribution of the Ulfberht swords it seems likely that they were made somewhere in the Rhineland area (which in later centuries became famous for its swordsmiths), and that they were imported into Scandinavia through Hedeby. A second group of marked blades, the Inglerii swords, began to appear in Scandinavia in the tenth century; it is thought that these were of Frankish origin. It is not known whether the older pattern-welded blades were also imports, and if so from where they came; nor is it yet known whether there were any centres in Scandinavia itself where specialist smiths produced fine weapons in any quantity. Simpler weapons with less perfect blades must surely have been produced at home from native lake-iron ores, for the Vikings can hardly have relied on imports for the great mass of their swords.

Imported blades arrived in Scandinavia without hilts (a group of such hiltless blades was found in Hedeby), and there they were fitted out according to whatever pattern was in fashion at the time and in the area where the buyer lived. Hilts of the Viking period can be classified into many types according to the shape of their pommel and guards, and several of these are definitely associated with particular areas and periods. The decoration on pommel and guard also varied; the earlier ones are often thickly plated with silver or bronze and punched all over with a close pattern of small circles or crosses; in the ninth and tenth centuries some have flowing interlacings picked out in niello on silver, while others have a bold simple pattern of alternate strips of tin and copper; towards the end of the period some have geometrical figures inlaid in brass on tin plating and emphasized with copper wire. In general, the effect is bright and lively, but also practical; the swords of Vikings were not made to be kept as showpieces in kings' armouries, but to be worn and used by fighting men of every rank.

Naturally, only the metal parts of swords and their trappings have survived. The middle part of the hilt would be a grip of wood or horn or bone. The scabbard would usually be of wood, sometimes covered with leather, and always lined with something soft and rust-repellant – oiled leather, sheepskin, fur, or waxed cloth. In the earlier part of the period pictures show the scabbard worn high on the left side, on a strap passing across the body; later it was hung from a sword-belt at the waist.

The equipment of the Viking warrior was completed by a round shield.

A sword hilt.

This was of thinnish wooden boards held together at the back by an iron bar; the hand gripped this bar, the knuckles passing through a hole cut from the centre of the boards and protected by the iron boss. There was also a strap by which the shield could be slung round one's neck, leaving both hands free, and by which it was hung up when not in use. There might be leather covering the face of the shield and perhaps an iron rim round it, but it would never be weighed down with metal, for its efficiency depended on its being easy to wield rather than on its strength. For the same reason it was usually small; those that adorned the Gokstad ship were about a yard across, but those shown on pictures often seem smaller still. They were painted in plain colours, and apparently also sometimes divided into segments of contrasting colours in simple geometrical designs.

These were the ordinary shields for everyday use, not richly decorated, as they were destined to be soon hacked to pieces and destroyed. But there were also far more splendid ones to be seen decking the halls of kings and chieftains, great shields showing scenes from tales of gods and heroes, and enriched with gold plaques and precious stones. We hear of them through the verses of three ninth-century poets who received such shields as gifts, and in return, to celebrate the magnificence of the giver, composed long descriptions of the legends represented on them. Unfortunately, the poems do not tell us much about their actual appearance; the most we can gather is that each contained various groups of pictures telling the stories of several myths and legends, and that these pictures were painted or incised on the shield itself, rather than, for instance, stamped in metal and applied to it.

These then were the weapons of the Norsemen; descriptions of how they used them are easily found in the sagas, and there are even a few representations of warriors engaged in single combat, for instance on the brow of one of the Vendel helmets (see the illustration on p. 110), and also on Gotland Stones. In the first of these we see that both men had begun the fight by using thrusting-spears, and that each had succeeded in piercing the other's shield or mailcoat; but the shafts hang limp and twisted, to show that they have been shattered by a sword blow, and now the two men are fighting with swords only. The one whose shield is weighed down by the broken spear has dropped his guard and is about to receive a mortal blow.

In swordplay one did not try to parry with blade against blade, which would be sure to spoil the edge; instead, one tried to turn the blow by rapid movements of the shield, which was held well away from the body and kept constantly in motion. It was safest to take the force of the blow on the flat of the shield; to take it on the iron rim was more of a gamble – it might break the opponent's sword, but, if that failed, the shield would certainly itself be split. If the enemy's weapon became wedged in one's shield, a quick twisting movement might jerk it out of his hand or even break it. Thus the shield played a very active part in the fighting, but was itself extremely vulnerable. In formal duels each man could use three shields, taking up a fresh one when the first was hacked to pieces; elsewhere we read of men pausing by agreement to fetch themselves fresh shields.

The sword was almost always used for hacking blows, not thrusts. It weighed between two and three pounds, and was usually held in one hand only, though a bold fighter might well discard his shield or sling it on his back, and use both hands to deal a heavier stroke. Many could use a sword left-handed, changing hands quickly to bewilder their opponent or if their own arm was wounded. The favourite tactic was to aim a heavy swinging stroke against the head or to cut off a limb; as the Danish historian Saxo says: 'Of old, in the ordering of combats, men did not try to exchange their blows thick and fast; but there was a pause, and at the same time a definite succession in the striking, the contest being carried on with few strokes, but those terrible, so that honour was paid more to the mightiness than to the number of the blows.'

Saxo makes the fighting sound rather static, but saga descriptions correct that impression; on the contrary, as defensive armour was so light, agility and speed were essential to survival. There was much dodging, twisting and ducking, and great leaps sideways or backwards to avoid blows at the legs; the fighters' feet must have been in constant motion, like a boxer's, and good balance was vital. The sagas admiringly preserve the memory of acrobatic feats. *Eyrbyggja Saga* tells how a man named Steinthor saved a friend who had slipped on ice during a fight by running up and thrusting his own shield over him to turn a blow, while with the other hand he cut off the leg of his attacker, and, 'in one and the same moment', leaped up into the air so that a stroke aimed at him by another enemy passed harmlessly between his legs. *Njal's Saga* gives another fine example, also from a fight on ice: Njal's son Skarphedin sees enemies on the far side of a partly frozen river, runs full tilt

Swordsmen fighting; detail from a Gotland stone.

One of the animal-headed posts found at Oseberg.

Slab from a Danish sarcophagus in St Paul's churchyard, London, showing a lion and serpent entwined.

down the bank, leaps across the open water, lands on smooth ice, keeping his balance and sliding over it 'as fast as a bird'; he bears down on the enemy so fast that their leader had not time to put his helmet on before Skarphedin is upon him and has split his skull with an axe, sweeping away again before anyone can touch him; someone throws a shield at his legs to trip him, but he jumps over it, landing on his feet again, and slides away across the ice.

The technique of a pitched battle seems to have been little different from that of these combats between pairs or small groups of men. It would begin with an exchange of missiles – arrows, spears and stones – but soon the two hosts would come to close quarters for what was essentially a series of single combats. There were only the simplest attempts to co-ordinate bodies of men in any strategical formations. One was the defensive 'shield-wall' formed by picked warriors if the battle turned against them; they would gather in a tight circle, each man's shield touching his neighbour's, and would make a stand until the attack was beaten off, or until all were killed. Another strategy was called the 'swine-array'; it consisted of men marching to the attack in a wedge formation, of which the van was called 'the snout'; both the manoeuvre itself and the name for it must have been learnt centuries before from the Roman legions' *caput porcinum*, and Norse legend attributed its invention to Odin himself. But such devices played only a minor part; the issue turned on the fighting skill of the individual.

Viking weapons; note the eye-guard on the helmet.

The kings of the Viking Age did battle, for preference, on board ship in the sheltered waters of a fjord. The massed fleets would be manoeuvred towards each other by rowers, the masts having been lowered; some ships might have an iron framework lashed to the prow to act as a ram or to hinder boarding, and others might raise wooden screens at the sides to ward off arrows. Sometimes several ships would be lashed together to keep their prows in line and to provide a stable platform for the fighting. Battles would begin with arrows, stones, and spears, and then the ships would close in and grapple, and the boarding parties would fight hand to hand until, in the words of a poet gloating over the rout of Harald Fairhair's enemies at Hafrsfjord:

Those who were hurt hurled themselves under benches,
Left their rumps sticking up, rammed their heads on the keel.
The warriors so prudent, when pelted with stones,
Set their bucklers behind them to shine on their backs;
These fellows fled eastwards, through Jadar they flew,
From Hafrsfjord homewards, longing for mead.

In fighting among themselves the Scandinavians preferred open battles to the fortifying and besieging of strongholds, although they did raise ramparts round certain trading-centres and encampments. There are remarkable round forts on the Swedish island of Öland, but these date from an earlier period and were neither re-used nor imitated by the Vikings. But in their attacks on England and the Continent the Vikings naturally had to learn how to overcome fortified towns and bridges by the use of battering rams, catapults, wall-borers, scaling ladders, and similar devices, and how to protect themselves under wattle screens as they went into the attack. *The Anglo-Saxon Chronicle* records that they set up temporary fortified encampments of their own, and indeed many earthworks in France and England are known locally as 'Danes' Dykes' or 'Danes' Camps', but none has yet been proved beyond doubt to belong to the Viking raiders.

The greatest fortifications ever raised by Scandinavians is the complex system of earthworks known as the Danevirke, running for almost nine miles across the base of the Jutland peninsula, from the head of the Schlei fjord to the swamps by the river Treene. A Frankish chronicle states that it was begun in 808 on the orders of King Godfred of Denmark to defend his southern borders against Franks and Saxons, but recent archaeological research has proved that much of it is older, dating from c.737. Other sections date from a period after 968; the whole structure was repeatedly reinforced by the addition of various palisades and moats and parapets in the course of succeeding centuries. This great monument of defensive engineering was made necessary by the risk of Continental attacks on Denmark, and more particularly on the trading town of Hedeby, which lies just to the north of the defences; it is unparalleled elsewhere in Scandinavia.

Aerial view of
Trelleborg.

Denmark also contains the sites of four great military camps commanding sea and land routes: Trelleborg in the west of Zealand, Aggersborg half-way along the Limfjord in North Jutland, Fyrkat on a headland not far south of this, and Nonnebaken in the middle of what is now the town of Odense. Their exact dating is being reassessed; on grounds of general historical plausibility they used to be ascribed to the reign of either Svein Forkbeard (*d.*1016) or of Cnut the Great, but at present archaeologists are more inclined to place them earlier, in the period 950–1000. Analysis of timber by denrochronology (tree-ring dating) in 1979 gave the date as 981.

The outstanding feature of these camps is the amazing uniformity and precision of their construction. The plan of Trelleborg shows the main features at a glance: a perfectly circular rampart, pierced by four gateways; two roads exactly dividing the inner area into quarters, and a ring-road running alongside the rampart; four groups of four houses, each exactly alike in size and structure, and grouped into a perfect square. Beyond this inner area, and peculiar to Trelleborg alone, lies a second rampart forming an arc of a circle concentric with the first; it encloses an outer court in which stand 15 slightly smaller houses laid out radially, save for two that stand a little apart, flanking a roadway. This outer rampart did not need to form a

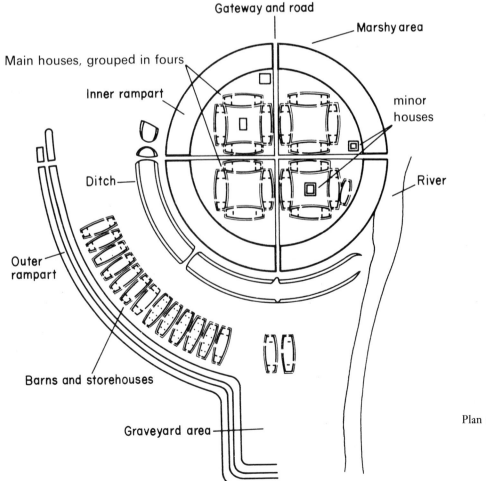

Plan of Trelleborg.

complete circle, for there were rivers and a lake to form natural defences; instead, it turned aside to enclose a rectangular area used as a burial ground, which probably existed before the camp was built.

The symmetry of Trelleborg is almost flawless; the three or four buildings in the inner area which do not fit into the pattern must have served special purposes – guardhouses near the gates, and possibly houses for the leaders. The surveying was done with mathematical exactness, using as unit of measurement the Roman foot of $11\frac{1}{2}$ inches. All the construction was carefully carried out; the roads were paved with wood; the ramparts, of uniform height and thickness, were strengthened internally with beams and externally with palisades; the gateways were roofed over, forming tunnels, and were closed by massive double doors, whose heavy keys and handles have been found where they had fallen.

The pattern to which the houses were built can be clearly traced from post-holes in the ground. The side walls were strongly curved inwards, the gable walls straight; inside, two partitions divided the house into one large central hall and two little end rooms, and these partitions incorporated sturdy posts to support the roof. There were four doors, one in each gable wall leading to the end rooms, and one in each side wall, both opening into the main hall. It is typical of the careful planning of these camps that when two houses stand side by side with a road between, their doors are not set facing each other, for fear that when everyone turned out at once in answer to a summons, two streams of men would jostle and hinder one another.

The men lived in the central hall, sitting and eating round the stone-lined hearth in the middle of the floor, and sleeping on a raised floor down the sides. If the fullest use was made of the space, some 75 men could live in each house; this is about the number which a smallish warship might normally carry, and it was once suggested that one house was allotted to each ship's company in the war-fleets of the Danish kings. The little end rooms seem to have been for stores of food and drink, sometimes kept in plank-lined pits dug in their floor; some presumably also held stores of arms. The houses in the outer court seem also to have been used for stores, or perhaps as working quarters; at any rate, only two of them had hearths, the mark of a dwelling.

Though the plan of the Trelleborg houses is clear, it is not certain of what material they were built. Their walls are defined by an inner row of shallow plank-holes set very close together, and an outer one of stout post-holes about a yard apart. These signs can be interpreted in different ways. One reconstruction proposes a tall house with plank walls, roofing of wooden shingles, and a row of posts supporting a curious gallery roof running right round the building. Another suggests that the space between the planks and the posts was filled with earth and turf to form a thick, low wall, as in Norwegian or Icelandic houses, and that the roof also was of turf and comparatively low. A third possibility is that the outer posts served as buttresses, set at an angle against the plank walls to help take the weight of the roof.

The three other camps closely resemble Trelleborg, except that they have

Reconstructed house at
Trelleborg: exterior.

Reconstructed house at
Trelleborg: interior.

no outer court or outer rampart. Fyrkat, though built on exactly the same plan as the main court of Trelleborg, is somewhat smaller, both in overall dimensions and in its actual houses, which were of the same shape. Much soil had been shifted to form a level area on which this camp could be built. Its rampart made up for being less thick by elaborate reinforcing timberwork and a high palisade. Its cemetery lay outside the camp and was approached by a special roadway leading to a raised platform, which may have served for funeral ceremonies; some of its burials are Christian, and some pagan, with rich grave-goods. Nonnebaken cannot be properly excavated because of the modern town above it. Aggersborg is by far the largest of them all, and contains three times as many houses, laid out in a more complex plan; each house is 110 Roman feet in length, as against 100 for the Trelleborg houses; the rampart is extremely massive, and its gates may have been crowned with wooden towers.

There can be no doubt that these camps were designed and built to serve the purpose of a powerful, well-organized monarchy, but their exact function (like their dating) is still debated. Paul Nørlund, the excavator of Trelleborg, argued that they were the headquarters of the mercenary armies gathered by Svein and Cnut for the invasion of England, and this theory won wide acceptance. However, as the suspected earlier dating is confirmed, it will have to be abandoned. There is also doubt as to how many men the camps actually housed; early estimates suggested that Fyrkat might hold about 800 men, Trelleborg 1,200, and Aggersborg perhaps as many as 3,000, even allowing for the fact that some buildings must have been storehouses rather than living quarters. But new excavations at Fyrkat show this is too high; of its 16 large buildings, four have both hearths and domestic objects, indicating that they were dwellings; four more have hearths but contained debris left by such trades as smithying and jewel-making; the remaining eight are hearthless, and so bare of finds that they can only have been barns, stables or storehouses. The distribution of finds at Trelleborg indicates a similar picture, in which case the notion of densely-populated barracks for invading armies seems less plausible. It is now thought that they served several functions simultaneously: as fortresses in a system of defence; as regional centres for royal administration; as refuges for the local population (comparable to, and possibly inspired by, the English *burhs* built by Alfred and Edward the Elder); as centres of production of goods for the use of the court; and as military camps as well, even if not on such a large scale as was once thought. The king at whose behest they were built may well have been Harald Bluetooth (d.985), who seems to have been a forceful personality with a taste for grandiose schemes, and who inscribed on a monumental stone the proud record of his reign – 'Harald, who won for himself Denmark and Norway and made the Danes Christian.' It is not known how long the camps remained in use, but probably not more than 20 or 30 years, since there is no trace of repairs to the timber of the houses. However, it is recorded that Aggersborg was 'sacked' in a peasants' revolt in 1086, so apparently it had been brought back into use to meet that emergency.

If the mathematical regularity of these camps is a fair indication of the spirit of those who organized them, the men must have been kept under very strict discipline. A memory of such military communities probably lies behind the largely fictional *Saga of the Jomsvikings*, about a band of warriors said to have been active in the Baltic in the late tenth century, and to have lived in a fortress under strict laws – no man could enrol among them who was under 18 or over 50, nor could any be accepted merely to please a kinsman; each must avenge the other as a brother; none must ever speak a word of fear; all booty was to be brought to the central pool; news must be given to the leader only; no woman must enter the camp; no man must be absent more than three nights; none must stir up quarrels, and even if one Jomsviking had formerly slain another's closest kinsman, the latter must take no vengeance but submit the matter to the leader's judgment. The fortress of the Jomsvikings, according to the saga, included a walled harbour that could hold three ships (or 300, according to a later text!); the entrance to the harbour was closed by iron gates set in a stone arch. The site of this fort, if it really existed, has not been identified.

Whether or not the Jomsvikings existed, there is no doubt that the late tenth century was a period during which the increasingly centralized authority of the Scandinavian kings was reflected in systematic and well-organized military undertakings. It was the period during which Hedeby, Birka, and Aarhus were fortified and the later phase of work on the Danevirke was begun; underwater defence-systems, in the form of palisades, barriers and blockages, some dating to the tenth century and others to the eleventh, have been found in the channels leading to Birka, at Hedeby harbour, and in several Danish fjords – the barrage of sunken ships in Roskilde Fjord being the most dramatic instance. It is clear that as the Viking Age progressed, firm organization and strategic thinking became more and more marked; the large mercenary armies of Svein and Cnut, recruited from all over Scandinavia, were the outcome of several generations of increasing skill in the arts of military planning.

7

The Family and Society

Family ties were of the utmost importance among Vikings; men took pride in their ancestors, reckoning up their genealogies through many generations, and had a strong sense of what was due from one kinsman to another. A family (defined fairly broadly, to include uncles and cousins) formed a close-knit group whose members stood by one another in all difficulties and avenged injuries done to any one of them. Their corporate sense of honour was strong; an insult to one was an insult to all, and, conversely, the disgrace incurred by a coward, a traitor, or a shameful criminal involved all his kinsfolk. There was also corporate responsibility: if a man had unjustifiably slain another, blood-money would often be paid not only by the killer but by his close kinsmen (the proportion contributed by each being decided by local custom), and it would be shared out in similar proportion between the victim's kin. Thus it was to the family's interest to curb the violence of unruly members before too much damage was done, even if afterwards honour demanded that the wrongdoer should be helped as far as possible.

Yet at the same time family authority did not crush independence and enterprise, so long as honour was not endangered; sons were free to follow their own way of life, whether at home or abroad. Families provided help and counsel, but were never an overpowering authority before which individuals must bow.

The status of women is difficult to assess. The lawcodes of all four Scandinavian lands reveal various social disadvantages: a woman could not vote at the Thing, nor be a judge, nor conduct a lawsuit on her own behalf; if she had brothers, she could not inherit from her parents (though she of course had a dowry from them at marriage), nor could she then share the blood-money if her father was killed; blood-money for her husband went to his kinsmen (including his children) but not to her; she could own property, but needed the approval of father, husband or male guardian to sell or buy anything above a very low value; her marriage was primarily a bargain arranged by the men of both families, for which her consent was not essential. On the other hand, a married woman's property did remain legally hers, however controlled her use of it might be; her husband could not dispose of it, and if the marriage ended in divorce all her property, even the dowry, returned with her to her own family. A widow was more independent still; she could manage her own property and that of her young children, and refuse a second marriage if she so wished. Women in medieval Europe would have envied Viking women these rights.

The legal evidence, however, is only part of the picture. Literary sources show women as vigorous and outspoken, respected by men and mingling freely with them; this impression is confirmed by contemporary Arab observers, who express surprise at the free and independent attitudes of Viking women. At home they had complete authority in household matters, and must often have run farms single-handed while their husbands were abroad. They could not conduct lawsuits, but, if sagas are to be believed, their implacable energy kept many a blood-feud alive when the men would gladly have ended it. There are even accounts of women wielding personal power, such as Aud the Deep-Minded, widow of a Viking king in Ireland, who led the emigration of her family and dependants by way of the Orkneys and Faroes to Iceland, and who apportioned land among them like a chieftain. Later, the Swedish rune-stones also bear witness to women's wealth and initiative, in inscriptions recording that a bereaved wife or daughter ordered their erection, and had commemorative causeways and bridges made (p. 107). Others of these stones were actually raised in honour of women; one such has been quoted already (p. 107), and another, of most elegant design, was set up by a man to commemorate his wife Odindisa – 'Never shall there come to Hassmyra a better housewife to care for the farm'.

A legal wife was distinguished from a concubine (of whom rich men had many) by the 'bride-price' which her husband had paid for her; normally she also received a dowry from her father and a gift from her husband on the day after the wedding. The first and third of these sums became her own property, and the dowry was repaid if the marriage ended in divorce. For a valid wedding there must also be a solemn drinking of 'bridal ale' before witnesses, and the man must be led by witnesses to the wife's bed. But a wife kept her name and patronymic, and never broke her links with her kinsmen; if a feud arose between them and her husband, it seems she might choose either side according to the merits of the case – indeed, two heroines in the cycle of legends about the Volsungs are praised for personally taking a gruesome blood-vengeance on their husbands for the sake of their dead brothers.

Divorce was easy, carrying no stigma for the party who demanded it, whether wife or husband; all that was needed was a declaration before witnesses of the grounds of complaint, and of the intention to divorce. We have no proper list of acceptable grounds, as all allusions to such matters had been dropped from the law codes before they were written down in Christian times; among those that figure in sagas are impotence, the wearing of breeches by a wife and of an effeminate shirt by a husband, and a husband's friendliness towards the man who had killed his wife's brother.

The chief peculiarity in the system of inheritance was the *odal* law concerning land, according to which ownership of the ancestral homestead rested with the family jointly; at a father's death the eldest son would take it, but must pay compensation to his brothers for their share in it. This prevented uneconomic splitting of estates, and must have stimulated younger sons to found new farms by clearing fresh land or by emigrating; at the same time, as the current possessor could sell the land provided he offered first option to the co-owners, the system was less rigid than an entail. Other pieces of land, chattels, and silver would be divided among the nearest heirs, and the law codes give detailed rules for determining the order of inheritance and the mode of sharing. Unusually complex cases occasionally find permanent record; for instance, an inscribed rock at Hillersjö in Sweden explains how a woman named Geirlaug was heir to her own daughter, herself a remarried widow whose property was inherited from the son of her first marriage:

Read these runes! Geirmund married Geirlaug, then a maiden. Later they had a son, before Geirmund was drowned; afterwards, the son died. Then she had Gudrik as husband. . . . They then had children; of these only a girl lived; and she was called Inga, and Rognvald of Snottsa had her to wife. Afterwards he died, and their son too, and the mother [Inga] inherited from her son. Inga afterwards had Eirik as husband. Then she died. Then Geirlaug came into this inheritance after her daughter Inga. The poet Thorbjorn carved these runes.

Illegitimate children were numerous, as most men took advantage of their female slaves, and many also had established concubines. In a Norwegian law it is stated that a slave-woman's child is to be a slave, unless expressly given freedom; other bastards had certain legal rights, as for instance to receive a minor share of the blood-money for their father or brother, and to inherit a few objects of low value from their father. In practice, however,

Rune-stone to a good wife, from Fläkebo, Sweden.

The Hillersjö rune-stone.

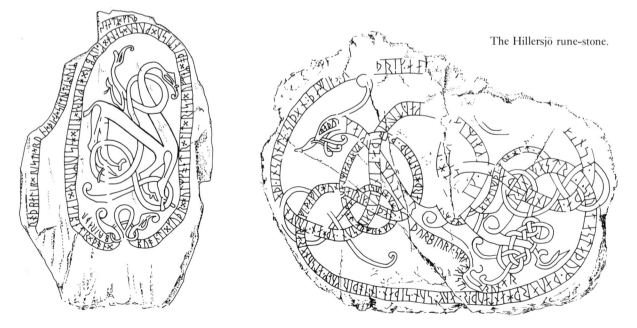

they were often treated more generously, and indeed the distinction between marriage and concubinage could become so blurred that the status of the children hardly suffered. In the royal house of Norway it happened more than once that an illegitimate son succeeded to the throne.

In any case, a bastard could be given full legal equality with legitimate children if his father adopted him. In Denmark and Sweden the procedure simply consisted in setting the child on the adopter's knee, and then publicly announcing the adoption at the Assembly. Norwegian laws contain a more colourful ceremony, which began by the adopter slaughtering a three-year-old ox and making a boot from the hide of its right leg; then he held a feast, during which the boot was set down in the middle of the hall, and first the child, then the adopter, then the rest of the family in turn, placed their right foot in it, thereby accepting the child as an equal member of their group. The boot was sometimes preserved as evidence.

A new-born baby had to be first shown to its father, who, if it was sickly or deformed, might order it to be exposed and left to die; the Arab at-Tartushi reports that poverty often drove the men of Hedeby to drown their infants. Masters might also order slaves' children to be exposed, to keep down the numbers in the household. But if the baby was to live, it was sprinkled with water – apparently a genuine heathen custom, not simply an imitation of baptism. Next, the father chose a name, preferably one carrying good luck, or one that had been borne by a recently dead kinsman, often an uncle or grandfather of the baby; certain gods' names (especially that of Thor) were much used as prefixes, originally as a sign that the child was placed under divine protection. Scandinavians used personal names and patronymics only (e.g. 'Helgi Thorstein's son', or 'Thora Thorstein's daughter'); there were no surnames in the modern sense, though certain royal or aristocratic families might have a collective name denoting descent from a famous ancestor. To distinguish an individual bearing a common name, it was usual to add a nickname; this, however, would normally only be given later in life,

Frame of a bed, from Oseberg.

and would allude to adult physical appearance or character, or to a definite incident, whether praiseworthy or ridiculous. Meanwhile, the baby would receive a gift to celebrate the name-giving, and later another for the cutting of his first tooth; the giving of a nickname might also be the occasion for a gift, if it was intended as a compliment.

Children were usually brought up at home, but it was fairly common for a boy to pass part of his childhood as a foster-son in another household. Far from being a sign of poverty, the arrangement was designed to forge honourable bonds between the two families; in feuds and other difficulties the boy would be able to claim the same degree of help from his foster-family as from his own kin, would have corresponding duties towards them, and would remain on particularly affectionate terms with them for the rest of his life.

In heathen times there was no education in the formal sense, and even later, Christian schools were few and extremely small. Children learnt farming and other crafts by the simple process of sharing household tasks to the best of their abilities, and practised fighting skills upon one another or their elders. Presumably a child who showed a talent for some specialized craft would be sent to learn it in another household if it did not run in his own family; knowledge of law, history and poetic technique must have been passed on in the same way, but there is no hint that learned men and famous poets gathered any formal groups of pupils round them.

Youngsters were expected to work hard; nobody was more despised than the 'charcoal-chewer', the boy who obstinately hung round the cooking-hearth when everyone else was out in the fields. They were also expected to show a bold spirit, and if this took the form of standing up to their elders, they were rather admired for it; it is no reproach if a saga-writer says of someone: 'he was a difficult boy to deal with, strong-willed and quarrelsome'.

Snorri tells an amusing story of how St Olaf, already a famous warrior and King of Norway, tested his three little half-brothers by sitting them on his knee and making hideous faces at them; the older two were terrified, but the three-year-old Harald glared back fiercely, and gave Olaf's moustache a forceful tug, at which Olaf remarked approvingly: 'You will be revengeful one day, kinsman.' Next day, the king and his mother Asta found the three boys playing by a pond; Halfdan and Guttorm were making model farms, but Harald was floating splinters of wood which he called 'warships'.

> Then the king called Halfdan and Guttorm to him, and first he asked Guttorm: 'What would you most like to have?'
>
> 'A cornfield,' he answered.
>
> 'And how big would you like your cornfield to be?'
>
> 'I would like to have the whole headland jutting out into the lake sown with corn every summer.'
>
> Now there are ten farmsteads on that headland, so the king answered: 'There would be a great deal of corn there.'

Then the king turned to Halfdan and asked: 'And what would you most like to have?'

'Cows,' he answered.

'How many would you like to have?' said the king.

'I would like,' said he, 'to have so many that when they went down to the lake to drink they would be standing all the way round the lake, as closely packed as they could stand.'

'That would be setting up house on a large scale,' said the king, 'and you take after your father in this.'

Then the king said to Harald: 'And what would you most like to have?'

'Warriors for my household,' he answered.

'And how many would you like to have?' said the king.

'I would like,' said he, 'to have so many that they would eat up my brother Halfdan's cows at a single meal.'

The king laughed, and said to Asta: 'You are bringing up a king here, mother.'

(In which he was right, for this boy grew up to be King Harald Hardradi, whose adventurous life ended in England in 1066, at the battle of Stamford Bridge.)

The existing lawcodes, written down in the twelfth century, say that a boy became an adult at 15 or at 16; however, it is very likely that in earlier times adulthood began at 12. Normally he would stay at home a few years longer, but sometimes he might go on a Viking expedition even at this early age; for instance, St Olaf was only 12 when he joined a ship commanded by his foster-father, and in the course of his teens (which he spent in continuous raiding) he himself became a leader. Most young men, after gathering wealth in years of roving, returned home to a life of farming; local conditions would determine whether a married son remained in his father's house, or built a new one beside it (as at Jarlshof), or moved some miles away (as was usual in Iceland). Many, of course, chose new settlements overseas and were joined there by their kinsmen; others spent the great part of their lives as fighting-men in the service of one leader or another, and never returned to farming. Others again spent their lives as craftsmen living in towns, as traders, or as travelling pedlars and blacksmiths.

Important though the family certainly was, other relationships also played a part in Viking life. That between chieftain and follower will be described below; there were also mutual obligations between host and guest, and those which a gift imposed on him who received it. In Scandinavia, as in ancient Greece, the giving of gifts implied far more than mere politeness: it set the seal on mutual relationships (lord and follower, host and guest, friend and friend); it conferred honour on the receiver, and obliged him to make a suitable response, either by giving some material object in exchange, or, more usually, by offering protection, help or loyalty to the giver – for, according to a Norse proverb, 'a gift always looks for a return'.

Friendship was much valued; those who so wished could give it the same permanent binding force as a blood-tie by the ceremonial swearing of blood-brotherhood. The actual Norse term is 'foster-brotherhood', but this is a figure of speech; the relationship was entered into by adults, though it resembled that between a child and his foster-family in so far as it established bonds equivalent to those of kinship. There are several accounts of the ceremony: the best is in *The Saga of Gisli*:

> They cut a 'neck-ring' of turf from the ground [i.e. a long strip forming an almost complete circle], and raised it up in such a way that the two ends were still fast, and under it they set an inlaid spear, tall enough for a man to lay his hand just on the rivets of the socket. The four of them were to pass underneath it. . . . Now they drew blood, and let their blood run together into earth scraped up from under the turf-ring; they mixed all this together, both earth and blood. After this they all fell on their knees and swore an oath that each would avenge the other like his own brother, and they called all the gods to witness this. And as they were all about to clasp hands . . .

The symbolism is plain: the arched loop of turf represents the womb of Mother Earth, through which the friends pass to be reborn as brothers; they mingle their blood in the earth as a sign that they are now 'of one blood', and they make the main obligation of their new relationship explicit by taking an oath, and confirm it by the hand-clasp which seals all bargains.

Such were the chief links binding a man to the immediate circle of his equals, his family and friends. At the same time, although Viking society was far from being as strongly stratified as that of many other cultures, the individual took his place in a simple social hierarchy. In the past there has sometimes been a rather naïve tendency to depict Viking life as a democratic idyll, regulated only by the joint decisions of all free men, expressed through the debates and judgments of the Things (Assemblies); in fact, as will be seen below, the legal and political decisions of the Things were firmly in the hands of local chieftains, and power rather than abstract justice determined the outcome of disputes. There is certainly a striking contrast between Scandinavia and the extreme social inequalities of feudal Europe, and equally certainly the average Viking was in many ways an enterprising individualist; nevertheless, this was not a world in which all men were equal.

There is indeed one Icelandic poem, *Rigsthula*, which is entirely devoted to class distinctions and their origins. It tells how a god named Rig wanders through the world and visits three homes, in each of which he shares board and bed with the master and mistress of the house, and begets a son who becomes ancestor to a whole class of men. The first house is a mere hovel, where food is coarse-ground husk-filled bread and simple broth; the son begotten there is named Thrall:

> *Wrinkled hands and knobbly knuckles,*
> *Fingers thick and face foul-looking,*
> *Back bowed down, and big flat feet.*

Goldfoil charms, showing a man and woman embracing.

This Thrall marries Bondmaid, whose looks match his own, and their hordes of children are born to be toilers:

> *They built fences, manured meadows,*
> *'Twas their task to tend the swine,*
> *Guard the goats, and dig up peat . . .*
> *From them is sprung the race of serfs.*

Next, Rig visits a well-built house, where the sturdy well-dressed master is making a loom, while his wife sits spinning, in smock and jewels; there Rig eats stewed calf and dainty foods, and there he begets a rosy-cheeked boy named Freeman, who takes to the farmer's life:

> *Taming oxen, making plough-frames,*
> *Raising house-beams, building barns,*
> *Making carts and driving ploughs.*

Freeman marries Daughter-in-Law, who wears a linen dress and goatskin kirtle and carries a bunch of housewife's keys; their sons bear such names as Fighter, Retainer, Farmer, Householder, Smith and Yeoman, and 'from them is sprung the race of freemen'.

Finally, Rig comes to a great hall where a very richly dressed man and woman sit idle, gazing into one another's eyes; there he is served with wheaten bread, roast pork and game-birds in silver dishes, and drinks wine from a silver-mounted tankard. The son he begets there is named Earl:

> *Blond his hair and bright his cheeks,*
> *Eyes as fierce as a young serpent's.*
> *Earl grew up in that same hall*
> *To shake a spear-shaft, string a bow,*
> *Bend the elm-bough, fashion arrows,*
> *Let a dart fly, fling a javelin,*
> *Ride on horseback, hunt with hounds,*
> *Brandish swords, do feats of swimming.*

Rig himself reappears to teach this fine youth wisdom, calls him his son, and urges him to win land to be a domain for his heirs; so Earl goes to war, wins estates, and obtains wealth to distribute among his followers. Then Earl marries a maiden of noble birth, and begets sons with such names as Heir, Offspring, and Youth. Of these sons, the youngest is named Kon ('Kon the Young' forms a pun on *konungr*, 'king'); he in turn becomes Rig's favourite and learns runic secrets from him, and, though the poem is unfortunately incomplete, it is clear enough that Kon is destined to surpass his father's splendour and become a king.

There is dispute over the date of this poem, some scholars seeing it as a tenth-century work embodying genuine Viking Age ideas, and others thinking it a much later invention, without traditional roots. Broadly speaking, its threefold division of men into slaves, yeoman-farmers, and an aristocratic class including earls and kings, does correspond to important

groupings in Viking society; on the other hand, it certainly falsifies the picture by suggesting that these divisions were sharper and more rigid than they can possibly have been, and by implying that they were perpetuated from generation to generation.

In reality, the period must have been one of considerable social mobility. Even at the bottom of the scale, among the slaves, it was not uncommon for men to be given freedom and allowed to set up small households of their own; moreover, the Vikings must have realized perfectly well that it was not heredity or a divine decree that made men and their descendants slaves, but the bad luck of capture in a raid. Among free men, there were many ways to improve one's lot: landless men could settle overseas; there was wealth to be won by plundering or by serving kings for pay; there were profits to be made by craftsmanship and trade. Curiously, *Rigsthula* does not mention the merchant; one would not expect to find him counted as a separate social rank, but it would have been appropriate to give him a place among the sons of Freeman. As it is, since 'Merchant' and 'Viking' are missing, the poem presents too static a picture, omitting two major ways of winning the wealth which, here as elsewhere, was the key to rising in the world. A man who had wealth and land, if he also had a forceful character, might well become a local leader with followers who looked to him for protection; in due time he or his sons would cross the rather nebulous borderline between the class of rich farmers and that of the local chieftains – men who differed only in scale, not in essence, from earls and even kings.

Moreover, there was a fundamental difference between Scandinavian society and the feudalism which was developing elsewhere in Europe, namely that here every man who owned land held it in absolute freehold, unencumbered by any dues or duties to an overlord. True, he might need a chieftain's protection if he became involved in disputes with his neighbours, and he would be expected to give that chieftain loyal help by fighting for him in his feuds, and in war. But the bond remained a personal one, and a dissatisfied follower could transfer his allegiance to another chieftain – possibly at some risk and inconvenience to himself, but without the dire penalties which would befall a feudal vassal who defied his overlord. A chieftain was expected to deal out justice between his followers, back them up in any disputes with outsiders, reward them generously for any service they gave him, and, if they followed him on raids, to share out the spoils and lands among them. If he failed in these duties, or if he lacked the personal arts of leadership, then, however aristocratic his ancestry might be, he would soon see his followers turning to some more effective rival.

The standing of chieftains varied greatly, from minor local leaders whose power was limited to a single fjord, to those who drew followers from a whole region, maintained a body of personal retainers, owned ships of war, and could claim the title of earl or even king. The term 'king' was elastic. In early times it meant no more than that one petty chieftain had been chosen by the rest to be their leader, but he remained dependent on their backing and on the decision of the local Things. There was no coronation; the

Rider with hawk and hound, from a Gotland stone.

essential formality was the king's appearance at the Thing, to receive oaths of loyalty and himself swear to rule justly. Gradually, however, strong kings imposed their authority upon more and more regions (often against persistent opposition), till at last each of the Scandinavian homelands was ruled by a single dynasty capable of forging it into a political and religious unity. Nevertheless, many earls remained extremely powerful; indeed, in Norway, the Earls of Hladir were always potential rivals to the king, and at times the actual rulers of the country.

In the settlements, arrangements varied. Iceland deliberately rejected kingship, since some of the leading settlers had bitterly resented Harald Fairhair's ambition to bring all Norway under his rule; instead, the Icelanders entrusted power to 36 chieftains of theoretically equal standing. The Orkneys were ruled by a dynasty of earls whose power sometimes extended also to Scotland and Man, but who owed a rather vague allegiance to the King of Norway. In Ireland and England there was a multiplicity of chieftains, sometimes calling themselves kings and sometimes not, whose spheres of influence fluctuated from decade to decade. Clearly, *Rigsthula* shows good judgment in reckoning Kon the king as only one, albeit the most glorious, among the sons of Earl, rather than giving him a separate divine ancestry.

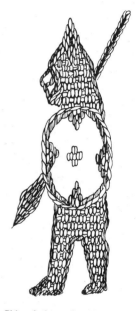

One mark of an earl or king was that he would maintain in his household a group of men bound to him by closer ties than his ordinary followers. These were his retainers, whose basic obligation was to fight for him whenever he needed them; meanwhile, they lived on his bounty, and at the end of their service were given land or gold or stocks of merchandise. Some might remain only a year or two, young men seeking adventure, booty, and the fame of having been for a while part of a great lord's retinue; others might spend the greater part of their lives there, forming the nucleus of a court. The deep personal loyalties created by this relationship were very powerful; indeed, the heroic devotion of retainers dying in battle beside their lord is one of the basic themes in Nordic and Germanic literature. The generosity of the lord to his men was also often a theme for poetry; a poet at Harald Fairhair's court paints a glowing picture of the life his warriors lead:

Skin-clad warrior, from the Oseberg Tapestry.

> They are favoured with wealth and finest sword-blades,
> With metal from Hunland and maids from the East;
> Glad are they then when they guess battle's near,
> Swift to leap up and lay hands to the oars,
> To snap off the grummets and splinter the tholes,
> And smite billows bravely at their lord's bidding.

Poets as well as warriors receive fine gifts from the king:

> One may see by their gear and their golden rings
> They are comrades close to the king;
> Red are their cloaks, with richly wrought borders,
> Swords bound with silver, corselets of ring-mail,

Belt-straps gilded, and helmets graven;
On their wrists are the rings which Harald gave them.

According to the same poet, Harald's court included a company of picked fighters on whom he particularly relied – the berserks, also known as 'wolf-skins'. From many texts it appears that there was an aura of mystery and horror surrounding such men; according to Snorri, they were devotees of Odin, from whom they derived their power, and they fought naked, filled with animal fury:

> They advanced without mail-coats, and were as frenzied as dogs or wolves; they bit their shields; they were as strong as bears or boars; they struck men down, but neither fire nor steel could mark them. This was called the Berserk Rage.

The name 'berserk' means 'bear-shirt' and not, as one might be tempted to think from Snorri's account, 'bare-shirt', i.e. naked; both this and the alternative name 'wolf-skin' imply that the men were clad in animal skins, or even that they were believed to change themselves into animals at will, like werewolves. This idea and that of the invulnerable naked champion seem both to be reflected in a pre-Viking Swedish representation of two figures,

Dies for stamping the decorative plaques on seventh-century Swedish helmets; warriors are shown marching, subduing monsters, and enacting the parts of 'berserk' and 'wolf-skin'.

one naked save for a belt and a horned helmet, and the other apparently human but wearing a wolf's pelt, including the head as a mask; they seem to be engaged in a ritual dance or combat. A naked warrior of similar type is also represented on an Anglo-Saxon sword-belt buckle of the seventh century – one more instance of motifs shared by Anglo-Saxons and Scandinavians in the generations immediately preceding the Viking Age. Later, the Oseberg Tapestry shows warriors wrapped in an odd hooded garment, which may be meant as a bearskin.

Many kings, historical or legendary, are said to have had berserks in their households; the reality behind such tales probably was the existence of fraternities of dedicated warriors, initiates of the cult of Odin, whose fighting frenzy may have been stimulated by rhythmic howling and leaping (as described in certain sagas), and similar methods of self-hypnosis. So long as they served a strong ruler they fulfilled a useful function, but without this control their ferocity and disregard for normal laws made them a menace; for this reason in later sagas they are sometimes represented as admirable champions, but more often as brutal bullies who terrorize everybody until they are routed by the saga hero.

In the course of time, as the monarchy developed, this simple and ancient form of court became more highly organized, with retainers of various ranks forming the king's Council and providing an armed guard round him day and night, or travelling the country to uphold his authority, gather taxes, and represent him at local Things. The surviving detailed accounts refer to thirteenth-century Norway, but already in the times of St Olaf or of Cnut the Great the courts had been much elaborated. In summer, the king and his retinue travelled the country, presiding and delivering judgments at the Things; in winter they chiefly lived on the king's estates, unless they were invited to other great lords' homes for the winter feasts.

We know little about how the trading-centres fitted into the pattern of social power. In early times they were presumably under the control of the local chieftain, as was the case in Iceland where, as soon as a ship came to land, the nearest chieftain would arrive and lay down terms of trade between the merchants and the farmers. However, it cannot be a coincidence that Kaupang, Helgö and Birka are all near the centres of royal power, and that several bitter conflicts between kings and lesser chieftains in more remote districts arose from the kings' claims to take control of trade into their own hands. Apparently the main trading-centres were supervised by a representative of the king, such as the man from whom St Anskar obtained permission to preach when he came to Birka. He presumably levied a toll on the merchants, in return for which the king must have guaranteed peace and law during the time of trading (a necessary precaution, among men gathering from many regions); probably the king also played a major part in maintaining the defences against raiders. There are signs that in some towns merchants were already beginning to organize themselves into guilds and lay down rules for fair trading; it is also known that travelling merchants formed guilds for their mutual defence and support.

Anglo-Saxon buckle from Finglesham, showing the Scandinavian motif of a naked spearman in horned helmet.

It was one of the basic underlying assumptions of the Scandinavian world that sooner or later anybody might find himself involved in a blood-feud; the whole network of relationships into which a man entered – relationships of blood, fostering, friendship, marriage, and allegiance to a chieftain – were designed to strengthen his hand when such a conflict arose. How this worked out in practice can best be seen by studying the course of a typical feud, such as forms the subject of so many Icelandic sagas.

The initial dispute might perhaps be over some quite minor matter which both sides at first seemed to take lightly, so that it could be long before the enmity came into the open; sooner or later, however, a member of one family would insult the other by word or blow, and honour would then be involved. The prudent and peaceful course would be for the victim to demand money in compensation, which only very arrogant and unjust men would refuse; many victims, however, thought it more manly to seek vengeance by bloodshed. The feud would escalate rapidly, as it was unthinkable for one kinsman to let another be slain without killing at least one person in retaliation – not necessarily the actual slayer, for, as a Norwegian lawcode puts it:

> It is an evil custom which has long existed in this land that, when a man has been slain, his kinsmen will attack whichever of the slayer's kin is considered the finest man (even though the killing may have been done without his knowledge or wish, and without his sharing in the deed), and they will not take vengeance on the slayer, even though this might easily be done.

Thus vengeance led to counter-vengeance, sometimes culminating in a large-scale fight between both families accompanied by their friends and dependents, or in such drastic deeds as a 'burning-in', when one party caught the others in their home, setting it on fire and leaving the adult males no choice but to burn to death or come out to face overwhelming odds. Eventually, through exhaustion or because the leaders on both sides were dead, the time would be ripe for a more peaceful settlement in which honour would be satisfied by blood-money rather than further bloodshed.

At this stage three courses were available: to grant 'sole judgment' to the injured party, to consult arbitrators, or to start a lawsuit. In the first case, one party acknowledged themselves in the wrong and appeased their opponent by asking him to assess whatever compensation he thought himself entitled to, and undertaking to abide by whatever penalties he imposed; custom and public opinion would restrain him from taking unfair advantage of the concession, but the satisfaction to his sense of honour made this form of settlement the most acceptable to an offended man.

In complex cases with rights and wrongs on both sides, the matter was often submitted to arbitrators, whose decision everyone swore to accept. The arbitrators would assess the compensation to which each party was entitled for injuries inflicted by the other. In this reckoning, equal injuries would be held to cancel each other out (flesh-wound being equal to flesh-

Men fighting, from a medieval Icelandic manuscript (*Flateyjarbók*).

wound, lost limb to lost limb, death to death), provided that the victims
were of roughly equal 'worth', i.e. of similar social standing; the death of a
servant in one party would not be held to cancel that of a householder in the
other, nor that of a farmer to cancel that of a chieftain's son. Another factor
in the reckoning would be provocation in words or blows; certain insults
were grave enough to justify any retaliation. When everything had been
taken into account, the arbitrators would strike a balance, declaring that one
side owed the other such-and-such sum in compensation for deaths and
injuries. There were basic scales of payment, determined by tradition; in
Iceland, for example, the price for a free man's life was 120 ounces of silver.
Alternatively, or additionally, the arbitrators could condemn a man to be
banished from the district or even from the country, either for a stated
number of years, or for life, or during the lifetime of his enemies; this was
partly meant as punishment, but mainly to prevent renewal of the feud. The
banished man would be allowed a convenient interval to set his affairs in
order and arrange his journey, during which time no one might molest him;
but if he failed to go, his enemies could attack him without risk of legal
penalties.

Men fighting: detail from a
Gotland stone.

The third course was to bring a lawsuit before an Assembly of the people,
known as a Thing. These were an essential feature of all Scandinavian
societies, acting both as law courts and as rudimentary Parliaments; all free
men owning more than a rather low minimum of property were expected to
attend, though in fact the decisions usually reflected the wishes of the most
powerful men present. There were small local Things for each district,
meeting at a fixed spot which often had some natural feature to recommend it
– a rock, hillock or burial mound from which the presiding chieftain and
other speakers could be clearly heard, or a circle of standing stones marking
the boundaries of the area. There were also regional Things to settle graver
problems, and in about 920 Iceland organized the Althing, an annual
General Assembly for the whole country. Usually the Things met at fixed
seasons, but they could also be summoned to debate urgent matters of
public policy; for instance, it lay with them to accept or reject a claimant to
the throne, or a proposed change of religion in their region. They could also
make new laws, and in Iceland at any rate it was customary for a man called
the Law-Speaker to recite one-third of the code at the Althing every year,
thus ensuring that traditional laws were not forgotten. There was a 'lawman'
with similar duties for each province in Sweden, and committees of
'lawmen' in Denmark and the Danelaw settlements. Such men, we learn
from the sagas, taught younger men and boys the intricacies of legal
formulas and procedures. The existing written lawcodes sometimes still
show traces of the rhythmic alliterative phrasing which helped to fix the oral
laws in men's memories.

These gatherings played an important part in public life. They usually
lasted several days (the Icelandic Althing lasted two weeks), during which
time men camped in temporary buildings near the Assembly-place, or were
entertained in nearby farms; the occasion provided good opportunities for

sports, gossip, match-making and petty trading. The upkeep of the Assembly-place usually fell to some wealthy family near by; like road- and bridge-building, it was a form of public work reflecting credit on those who undertook it, so that several Swedish rune-stones proclaim names of those who had 'made a Thing-stead', or had embellished an existing site with avenues of standing-stones. Originally, a Thing was to some extent a religious gathering, 'hallowed' in the name of the gods, and the peace which all must keep during the lawsuits and debates was akin to the peace surrounding a sanctuary. According to *Egil's Saga*, one Norwegian law court in heathen times sat within a sacred enclosure:

> Where the court was held there was a level field, and hazel poles were set up in a circle in the field, with ropes running round all of them on the outer side; these were called the sanctuary bonds [literally, '*vé* bonds'; see p. 166]. Within the circle sat the judges, 12 from Firdafylki and 12 from Sygnafylki and 12 from Hordafylki, and these three dozen men were to pass judgment there on men's lawsuits.

The procedure for bringing a lawsuit before a Thing must have varied in different regions; that from Iceland is the best known, and will be outlined here. In a case of manslaying, the first step was for the victim's kinsmen to decide which of them would act as plaintiff, or, if none of them felt equal to the task (through lack of legal knowledge or of influential connections), to persuade someone else to act on their behalf. Next, the plaintiff must go to the slayer's home on a legally appointed day, proclaim the accusation against him before witnesses, and summon him to appear at the Thing. The identity of the slayer was rarely in doubt, since he had to announce the fact of the killing as soon as it had occurred – to fail to do so changed a simple manslaying to secret murder, the most shameful of crimes.

In the interval before the next Thing, both plaintiff and defendant would be busy rallying as much support as they could among their kinsmen and friends, and endeavouring to enlist the aid of a chieftain. If the two adversaries were followers of different chieftains, each could count almost automatically on being helped by his own one, but if both were followers of the same man, one or other of them would have to seek support elsewhere – unless of course they asked him to act as arbitrator, in the manner described above. Sometimes there would also be manoeuvring to get the case heard at one local Thing rather than another, as there was advantage in having the hearing in a district where one had many friends. If the parties in the suit were themselves chieftains, their efforts would be directed towards gathering the maximum number of armed followers to accompany them to the Thing.

Reaching the Thing might itself be a problem; one's opponents might try to bar the way by force, since whoever failed to appear was considered to have lost his case. Once there, plaintiff and defendant had to frame their pleas through intricate legal formulas (one slip in reciting which could destroy their chances), and each had to produce 'witnesses' – not in the modern sense, but simply neighbours prepared to swear that in their opinion what was said was true, and that each step in the legal procedure had been correctly carried out. The pleas were heard by a bench of 36 'judges' whose function was almost exactly that of a modern jury – not to conduct inquiries or bring superior legal knowledge to bear, but merely to give a verdict for one side or the other. These 'judges' were appointed by the presiding chieftains; at a local Icelandic Thing the three nearest chieftains would each choose 12 of them, but at the Althing a greater number of chieftains shared the task, each therefore appointing fewer judges, since the total was still 36. It was this fact which made it so vital for each party to have good backing. Lawsuits were indeed only a thinly disguised trial of strength between plaintiff and defendant, and if neither succeeded in tripping the other on some legal technicality, the judges would almost certainly be influenced by the support each side could muster, and especially by the known attitude of the chieftains. It was not unknown for the court to be overawed by an open display of force, despite all rules about keeping the peace, and to break up without giving a decision.

The plaintiff's plea was essentially a simple accusation of manslaying; the

Thingvellir, the meeting-place of the Icelandic Althing.

defendant sought to counter this by claiming that the dead man had given such provocation, by previous attacks or insults, that the killing was justified and no compensation or penalty should be exacted for it. If the judges accepted this plea, they declared that the dead man had been 'unholy' when he fell, and that his kinsmen could claim nothing for their loss. If on the other hand they found for the plaintiff, they might impose on the defendant the same type of banishment as arbitrators often did, but more usually they imposed the far graver penalty of full outlawry.

A man condemned to full outlawry had no legal rights left. His property was forfeit to the man who had sued him (with a share going to the court that had condemned him); anyone who so wished could kill him, without penalty, and his kinsmen would have no legal redress, though they might still take personal vengeance; theoretically, no one should help or shelter the outlaw, and his only hope was to flee the country, or to hide in forests and wild places and live by banditry. In practice, the outlook was less appalling. It was left to the man's personal enemies to see the sentence carried out, by coming with force to seize his homestead and his goods, and, if possible, kill him on the spot; if the plaintiff could not muster enough supporters to do this speedily, the outlaw might well be smuggled abroad by his friends, or take refuge in the house of a powerful protector, or even remain at home and rely on his local popularity to keep him safe. Of course, if the crime was one which had outraged public opinion there would be less chance of escape, (contemptible criminals such as thieves or dabblers in black magic were usually hunted down and executed summarily as soon as the verdict was passed); but a man condemned for ordinary manslaying might, by the help of kinsmen and friends, make a new life for himself elsewhere.

8
Games, Arts and Poetry

According to Tacitus, in Roman times the Germanic tribes had only one form of public entertainment, which was performed at all their gatherings – a dance, in which 'naked youths leap and bound between upturned spears'. This must surely have been a ritual honouring the war-god; something very like it was still remembered 600 years later, judging by Swedish and Anglo-Saxon figures of warriors in horned helmets, some naked, some clad, grasping spears and sometimes also a short sword, and apparently dancing, singly or in pairs. Particularly interesting are the men represented on p. 138; the 'berserk' is leaping vigorously with the help of his spears, while the 'wolf-skin' is about to draw his sword; their frozen gestures irresistibly suggest one moment in a ritual. But sagas mention no such customs in Viking times, either because they had died out, or possibly because they were so closely linked with the cult of Odin that Christian writers preferred to ignore them. Possibly, however, some faint memory of them lingered in a display given by Scandinavian mercenaries for the Byzantine Emperor Constantine VII as a Christmas entertainment: two companies danced in a ring, striking their shields with sticks and shouting 'Yule, Yule, Yule!', and in each company two men were dressed in furs and masks. One might also note the curious pose of a figure in the representation of Valhalla on one of the Gotland stones (see p. 181); he seems to be doing a back somersault over a horizontally held spear, which is held by another man lying flat on the ground. It is interesting to find this acrobatic display in a religious context.

But if warriors' rituals were almost forgotten in the Viking Age, warriors' skills were not. Time and again one reads of feats of strength and agility, and of popular sports requiring these qualities; wrestling, for instance, demanded great strength combined with nimbleness and cunning; in swimming, speed was less prized than the ability to drag one's opponent down and hold him under water till he collapsed, without oneself needing to come up for air. Obviously, the skills needed here were also useful in battle on land or sea, and the more violently such sports were played the better they were enjoyed. It is said that the outlaw Grettir once joined a group of wrestlers, allowed the two strongest to tackle him together, and handled them so roughly that all three were bruised and bloody – 'everyone thought it splendid sport, and thanked them for their wrestling when they ceased'. Even comparatively harmless ball-games were pretty roughly played, and

A twelfth-century tapestry from Skog church, Sweden. A church is being attacked by monsters, while men in a nearby bell-tower ring the bells to protect it; the scene symbolizes the conflict between Christianity and heathenism.

often ended in blows and a blood-feud (though here saga accounts may be misleading, for an episode that did not lead to trouble would be unlikely to figure in their plots).

This aggressiveness was inflamed by the fact that personal honour was so easily involved in success in such contests. This was even the case in the horse-fights so much loved in Norway and Iceland; the more fiercely a stallion kicked and bit, the greater his owner's glory. Horse-fighting was an ancient sport, shown on the sixth-century Swedish Häggeby Stone; originally it may have been part of the cult of the fertility-god Frey (to whom horses were sacred), and in more modern times it was associated with harvest festivals in Norway. In 1618 a Norwegian bishop wrote:

A crowd of people congregate on St. Bartholomew's Day with their horses, from all the district round, and the horses are set to bite each other two by two, the notion being that when they bite each other lustily there will be a good crop, and vice versa.

Sagas give a good picture of the Icelandic horse-fights. The stallions were led into a meadow where the crowds were gathered, and there were mares

tethered near by to rouse them; they were loosed in pairs, and beside each horse ran a man armed with a stout stick, to goad it if it began to yield ground. It was forbidden to use this stick against one's opponent's horse, but of course this rule was often broken. Typical is the episode in *The Saga of Thorstein of the Cudgel-Blow*:

Another section from the Skog tapestry. These three figures probably are Odin (one-eyed and holding an axe), Thor (holding a hammer), and Frey (holding a plant).

> Thorstein and Thord had arranged a fight between young stallions, and when they set them at each other it was Thord's stallion which was the less eager to bite. Then Thord struck Thorstein's stallion on the jaw, for he thought his own was getting the worst of it, and this was a heavy blow; but Thorstein saw it, and in reply he struck Thord's stallion a far heavier blow, and so now Thord's stallion ran away, and all the men yelled with excitement. Then Thord struck Thorstein with the cudgel he had used on the horses, and the blow caught him on the eyebrow, so that the flesh was torn and hung over the eye.

Icelandic horse-fights seem to have been held regularly at particular places and times, for instance after a legal Assembly, and sometimes other games also took place at the same meeting; on one occasion it is stated that

A horsefight, from a codex of Icelandic laws (*Jónsbók*, fourteenth century).

the competitors had been chosen to represent neighbouring districts. In Norway in later times district rivalry was acute; there, the horse-fights were followed by wild bareback races, the riders lashing one another as well as their mounts, and often making their horses leap on to a rock as a grand finale. Icelanders, on the contrary, do not seem to have raced much; references to betting on the outcome of these or any other sports are very rare.

It would, however, be wrong to imagine that Scandinavians only appreciated physical prowess and violent sports; on the contrary, the ideal man was expected to master a wide range of mental, verbal and artistic skills. Earl Rognvald of the Orkneys (1135–58) could boast of nine assorted

A horsefight; sixth-century Swedish rock carving.

talents, all traditional ones ascribed again and again, in varying combinations, to legendary or historical heroes:

> *There are nine skills known to me –*
> *At 'tables' I play ably;*
> *Rarely I run out of runes;*
> *Reading, smith-craft, both come ready;*
> *I can skim the ground on skis,*
> *Wield a bow, do well in rowing;*
> *To both arts I can bend my mind:*
> *Poet's lay and harper's playing.*

First on Rognvald's list is the ability to play 'tables'. This rather vague term referred to any game played on a marked board with round flattish pieces, and sometimes with dice; it is often translated 'draughts', but this is misleading, for modern draughts only reached Europe at the very end of the medieval period. Old Norse has various compound names for such games, suggesting that several varieties of 'tables' were known, but the texts throw little light on how they were played. Although gaming-pieces are among the commonest objects in Viking graves, it is unfortunately rarely possible to decide whether the set is complete. It is, however, almost certain that in one type of game 16 pieces of one colour played against eight pieces and a 'king' of another; other sets have two 'kings', others none.

Bone figurine from Iceland, found with 24 gaming-pieces; a 'king' for a board-game?

The finest gaming-board yet found comes from Balinderry, near Limerick; it is marked out by holes, seven by seven, and the 'pieces' were little bone pegs. The central hole and the corners are emphasized by circles, reminiscent of modern games of 'Fox and Geese' where the fox starts in the middle and a team of 10 or 12 geese tries to drive him into a corner. A Swedish rune-stone shows men playing on a similarly marked board, while a slate found at Jarlshof has a different but related pattern.

It is usually said that chess was unknown in northern Europe before about 1200, so that references ascribing it to the Viking Age must be anachronisms; however, a bone playing-piece recently found in York is shaped like an Arabic chess-castle, while its decoration looks like pre-Conquest Scandinavian work. Chessmen have also recently been found in Dublin. It would not be at all strange if the Vikings, thanks to their contacts with the Arab world, learnt this game earlier than other Europeans.

Rognvald's next boast, that knowledge of runes rarely fails him, opens up wide perspectives into Scandinavian culture, where the use of runes had both magical and practical importance. The early Germanic inscriptions in this alphabet, almost always brief and enigmatic, suggest religious or magic formulas; by the Viking Age the alphabet had been cut from 24 to 16 characters, and was freely used for normal secular purposes, e.g. for inscribing the owner's name on some valuable object, or (to judge by twelfth-century examples) for writing commercial records and personal letters on wooden tablets. Nevertheless, literary allusions show that much of the old aura of mystery still lingered. According to a stock poetic phrase,

runes were 'sprung from the divine powers'; according to mythological texts, they had been discovered by Odin himself at the price of many torments. One of the most striking passages in the *Poetic Edda* puts these words in Odin's mouth:

> *I know that I hung for nine whole nights*
> *   Upon a windswept tree,*
> *Gashed by a spear and given to Odin,*
> *   Myself given to myself,*
> *On the tree of which no man can tell*
> *   From what roots it has sprung.*
>
> *No man served me with bread or drink;*
> *   I peered down below,*
> *Took the runes up, shrieking took them,*
> *   Then fell back again.*

Gold brooches, silver arm-rings and Thor's hammer from Denmark; tenth century.

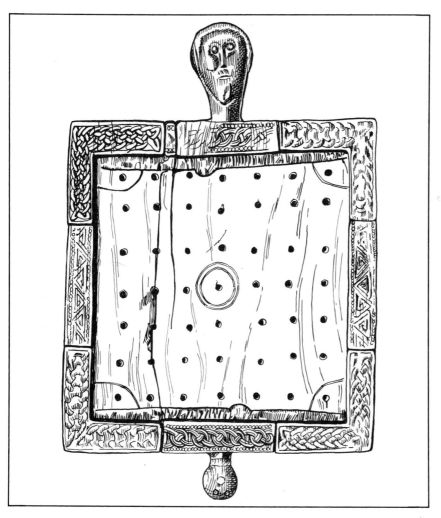

A Viking gaming-board, from Balinderry, Ireland.

Odin promises his follower power over runes:

You shall find runes and signs to read,
(Signs most mighty, signs most strong),
Which the soothsayer coloured, the high gods made,
And Hroptr of the gods had carved.

Do you know how they should be carved?
Do you know how they should be read?
Do you know how they should be coloured?
Do you know how they should be tried?

BELOW
A runic memorial stone, from
Risbyle, Uppland, Sweden.
RIGHT
A picture-stone from Lärbro,
Gotland; for the interpretation
of its scenes, see p. 180–81.

Another Eddic poem tells of a Valkyrie giving Sigurd the Dragon-Slayer instructions in the use of runes as magic signs – for victory, one should carve them on one's sword-hilts and twice name Tyr (an ancient war-god); to help a woman in labour, one should write some on her palms, bind others round her joints, and pray to the goddesses. Yet even here we are not told exactly what must be written – presumably only a few characters, perhaps symbolizing the supernatural beings to be invoked.

The alleged uses of rune-magic were numerous; according to *Rigsthula*:

> *The youthful Kon knew the runes,*
> *Runes everlasting, runes life-giving;*
> *Knew also how to save men's lives,*
> *Blunt the sword-blades, calm the billows;*
> *Could understand the cries of birds,*
> *Could quench the flames and quieten sorrows.*

The phrasing of Rognvald's poem strongly suggests that he had in mind this heathen magical tradition, and meant 'I am never at a loss for some runic spell to help me in a crisis', rather than simply 'I know my alphabet'.

But runes were also much used for everyday purposes, especially for cutting inscriptions on memorial stones, and this too was a skill of which men were proud; many a Swedish stone bears the name of the man who inscribed it as well as that of the man it commemorates, and a few challenge the passer-by with 'Let him read this who can!' On these stones the lettering is skilfully cut on snake-like bands; originally the design was also painted in contrasting colours (red, black, white and blue), so that the characters stood out clearly, and word-divisions were easy to see – a fact which may explain the reference to 'colouring' runes in the poem quoted above, though here too a magical colour-symbolism is possible.

Next, Rognvald mentions 'smith-craft', a term which naturally included all forms of metal-working, and also wood-carving, carpentry, bone-carving, and various other forms of handicraft. There were of course many specialist craftsmen earning their living by their work, and the high technical achievement of many Viking Age objects indicates that they were made by such men, but ordinary farmers and warriors would also turn their hands to metal-work and wood-work to meet household needs, or simply as a pleasant pastime.

The decorative impulse in Viking art was extremely strong; surfaces were covered with close and complex ornamentation which often, on close examination, is seen to be a semi-abstract pattern of intertwining animals whose distorted limbs and bodies twist and clutch at one another in a formal, rhythmic design. There are several distinct varieties of these animal patterns, and geometric ornament was also much used. The techniques were highly skilled in both wood and metal-working, producing results of amazing richness, accuracy and minuteness of detail, while at the same time the overall impression is both intricate and vigorous. Obviously, the finest pieces were produced by master-craftsmen for wealthy buyers; nevertheless, if more examples of furniture and utensils had survived, one might well have found that articles in everyday use were as amply (though probably not as skilfully) ornamented as those laid in the graves of the rich. A fine wooden panel with an animal design on it was found in Dublin in 1973, which may be part of a chair, chest or door; while from York in 1977 has come a carved piece of wood, probably the arm of a chair, studded with silver nails that held an inlay of some organic material, presumably leather. Certainly much woodwork even in ordinary houses was carved, especially the posts of the high-seats and the wall panelling; walls were also adorned with long narrow strips of tapestry forming a frieze around the room, in the same manner as the Bayeux Tapestry; benches were often covered with patterned cloths. Visually, the Viking world was gay and colourful.

Besides the abstract designs based on geometric or animal forms, the Vikings also had a tradition of simpler pictorial art, apparently always applied to subjects from myths, religious rituals, or heroic legends. The surviving examples are mostly the enduring stone-carvings of Gotland, Sweden or the Isle of Man; their scenes, where these can be identified, show the welcome of the dead to Valhalla, the myths of Thor and Odin, the exploits of Sigurd the Dragon-Slayer; and the unidentified ones are probably of the same type – though it is conceivable that some memorial stones might show scenes from the life of the dead man. We also know from literary references that shields and wall-panels could be painted or engraved with mythological scenes, and the superb Oseberg Tapestry (the interpretation of which is still conjectural) reminds us that narrative art in needlework was well known among Viking women. In the early eleventh century, the Norwegian King Olaf the Saint had in his hall a tapestry showing scenes from the ever-popular legend of Sigurd, which is described in a contemporary poem; the scenes shown were the same ones as on the surviving stones which illustrate Sigurd's story.

The Gotland picture-stones are particularly satisfying works of art. They are huge blocks, often 10–12 feet high, and cut to a characteristic mushroom shape; the figures, carved in very low relief, are usually laid out in orderly well-proportioned panels separated by bands of ornament. Originally the whole surface was painted over in various colours; the painting of the background has been restored, so that the figures should show up in silhouette, but details painted on the figures themselves are lost for ever, which increases the difficulties of interpretation.

The human figures on stone-carvings and tapestries are rather stylized, as are the faces on certain little metal pendants and other ornaments. But there are also a few heads, modelled in the round, whose features are realistic and indeed strongly individual – notably those on the frame of the Oseberg wagon and one from Sweden, carved on the end of a horn rod. Nor must one forget that the humour which is so marked in Norse literature occasionally comes out in art too, for instance in a set of 12 grotesque pendants whose exaggerated features, half human and half snake, are picked out in the most delicate silver filigree.

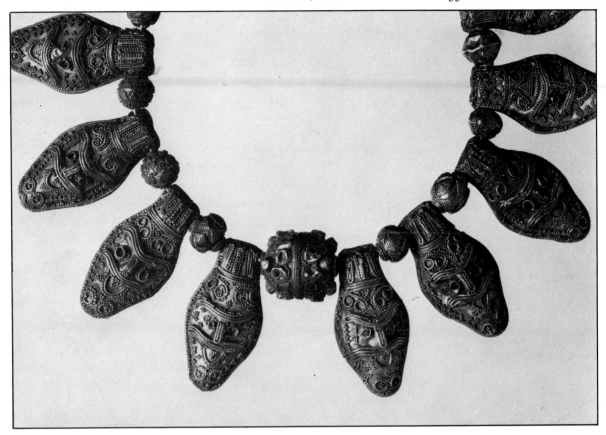

Necklace of silver filigree beads and pendants, from Gotland.

Verbal dexterity was highly prized; of the two last skills claimed by Rognvald, poetry and harping, the former would certainly be the more valued. A clever poet could grow rich by attaching himself to a king's household and composing highly-wrought poems in praise of his valour, for which he would be rewarded with rings, weapons, or other gifts. Icelanders showed particular aptitude for this, and many took service at foreign courts, sometimes for a few years, sometimes for life; their poems are often very valuable sources for the historian.

But these semi-professionals were not the only poets; many men could produce pithy eight-line stanzas commemorating a moment of triumph or danger in battle, threatening, mocking or cursing an enemy, praising a girl, lamenting a friend's death, or foreboding their own doom. And for each man who could compose poetry there were dozens who could appreciate it, even though its characteristic merits were scrupulous obedience to rigid metrical rules, intricate patterns of alliteration, assonance and internal rhyme, and a style in which persons and things were to be obliquely indicated through traditional, and especially mythological, allusions. In this style, for example, the statement 'the generous king gave me a gold arm-ring' might be conveyed by 'the scatterer of riches hung the burden of Grani upon the falcon's tree' – Grani being Sigurd's horse, laden with gold from the dragon's lair, and the 'falcon's tree' being the human forearm, on which tame birds were carried for the sport of hawking. This type of poetry is called scaldic (from *skáld*, a court poet); it can be traced as far back as, roughly, the mid-ninth century, and its occurrence on eleventh-century Swedish rune-stones shows that it was known there as well as in Norway and Iceland. Rognvald's own poem is an example of this almost untranslatable genre; the rendering of it on p. 149 manages the internal rhymes and half-rhymes, but breaks several rules governing metre and alliteration.

Far older and simpler is the type known as Eddic poetry (from the name of the manuscript containing it), though it does not follow that all surviving examples are equally old. Eddic poems are anonymous narratives or dialogues or collections of proverbs and religious lore; their subjects are either mythological or drawn from legends of ancient Germanic heroes, and often correspond closely with scenes popular in art.

Lays about heroes were being composed among many Germanic tribes at least as early as the fourth century, and by Viking times all Scandinavian peoples must have known such works, though the Icelanders were the only ones eventually to preserve some in writing. They were originally meant to be declaimed in chieftains' halls, possibly accompanied by the harp, and their proud tales of vengeance, loyalty, fate and death are the finest expression of the heroic ideals of this culture. Perhaps the most famous of all, both then and now, is the cycle about Sigurd the Volsung, who slew the dragon Fafnir to help a treacherous dwarf, and while roasting the dragon's

The exploits of Sigurd, on the Ramsund Rock, Sweden. The story runs from right to left: Sigurd kills the dragon (represented by the snake-headed band of runic writing); the treasure is laid on the horse; Sigurd roasts the dragon's heart, licks its blood from his thumb, and understands the two birds' speech; the treacherous Regin is decapitated.

heart, accidentally tasted its blood; he was at once able to understand the language of certain birds, who advised him to behead the dwarf and take the dragon's gold himself – a scene represented again and again in Viking art. Other lays show Sigurd entangled in a tragic conflict of loves and loyalties, with his wife Gudrun, the vengeful semi-Valkyrie Brynhild, and his friends and brothers-in-law Gunnar and Hogni, by whom he was treacherously slain. These two in turn are the heroes of another lay, telling how they were cruelly killed by Attila the Hun; Hogni's heart was cut out of his body, and Gunnar was cast into a snake-pit when he would not reveal the hiding-place of the dead Sigurd's treasure.

Whereas the heroic lays of the *Poetic Edda* are almost always tragic, the mythological ones are more varied in tone, ranging from lively accounts of Thor's encounters with giants or monsters to the personal tragedy of the death of Balder or the cosmic tragedy of the Doom of the Gods; others are not narratives at all, but collections of proverbial wisdom. On the whole, there is little to link these poems directly to the cult practices (as distinct from the stories) of heathen religion; they are designed for entertainment, not for worship. One particular type, consisting of questions and answers on points of mythological lore, might conceivably have originated from initiation ceremonies in which candidates had to prove their esoteric knowledge; yet even these probably survived simply as useful aids to understanding allusions in scaldic verse. A good example of this type is a poem telling how Odin and a giant put each other to the test with some 30 questions such as this:

> '*This one thing tell, if your wit holds good,*
>   *If you know it, O Vafthrudnir:*
> *Whence came the earth or the upper sky*
>   *At first, O learned ogre?*'

> '*From Ymir's flesh the earth was formed,*
>   *The boulders from his bones,*
> *The sky from the frost-cold giant's skull,*
>   *The billows from his blood.*'

Poetry, whether Eddic or scaldic, may not have been the only literary entertainment in chieftains' halls. There is a well-known anecdote about an impoverished Icelander who visited King Harald Hardradi:

The king asked him whether he had any learning, and he said he knew some sagas. Then the king said he would accept him at court, but that he would be bound to provide entertainment whenever it was wanted, whoever might ask him. And he did so, and became well liked at court, and the courtiers gave him clothes and the king bestowed weapons on him.

Towards Christmas the Icelander became gloomy, and confessed that he had told every story he knew, save one which he did not dare attempt – that of King Harald's own travels to Byzantium and the Holy Land. The king bade him tell it in small sections over the twelve days of Christmas, 'for there is always heavy drinking at Christmas, and it is only for a short while at a time that people would sit and listen to such entertainments'. At the end, he praised the Icelander's tale, and asked where he had learnt it; he replied that he had learnt it bit by bit at each annual Assembly in Iceland, from one of Harald's own former companions. The king rewarded him with a good stock of merchandise, so that he became prosperous.

Though this pleasing anecdote was only written in the thirteenth century, its picture of eleventh-century customs may well be accurate. However, there is not enough evidence to show whether the formal telling of sagas was a talent cultivated in the earlier Viking Age. Informal story-telling there must surely have been; genealogies were learnt, anecdotes about ancestors were remembered, news was constantly exchanged, witty sayings and clever verses were repeated (evidently accompanied by some account of the circumstances giving them their point), and, above all, the concern for personal fame ensured that the memory of a man's deeds was kept alive. This was of course particularly true of kings and great warriors, but the eagerness with which Icelanders fostered traditions about the first settlers shows that the same impulse was present at other levels of society. The existing Icelandic sagas, however, are written works of the twelfth and thirteenth centuries; often they contain information about events, customs

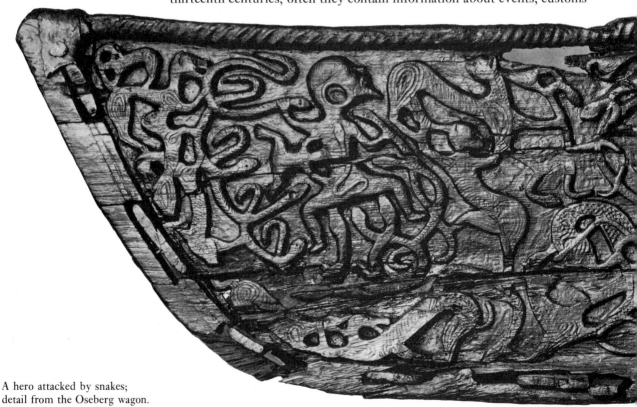

A hero attacked by snakes; detail from the Oseberg wagon.

and beliefs of the Viking Age, but they themselves are the artistic products of a later age and culture, and so beyond the scope of this book.

No account of the pleasurable aspects of Viking life would be complete without a mention of the feasts and drinking-sessions which were their most cherished pastime. These were mostly held in autumn and winter (when meat and ale were most easily available, and farm work was at a minimum), and they lasted for several days at a time. Besides the seasonal religious festivals such as that at mid-winter (Yule, later assimilated to Christmas), there were wedding feasts and funeral feasts and feasts for an heir taking up an inheritance – the latter being also to some extent a funeral feast, though sometimes several months after the actual burial.

The crucial element in the inheritance ceremony was the drinking, not the eating. According to Snorri, it was a custom in Norway early in the ninth century that the heir of a king or earl could not sit in his father's seat nor take full possession of his inheritance until he had drunk a solemn toast, standing, and made a vow to perform some noteworthy deeds. Such vows are several times mentioned; sometimes they were made while grasping a particular drinking-horn, or with one's foot placed on a particular plank or stone, or with one's hand laid on the bristles of a boar; sometimes several men swore, rivalling one another in the boldness of their undertakings.

There are descriptions of various drinking ceremonies. The liquor was kept in a large communal vessel, from which it was served out in horns;

Drinking scene: detail from a Gotland stone.

sometimes a single big horn went round, each man draining it dry in a toast before it was refilled and handed to his neighbour; sometimes two men, or a man and a woman, shared a horn between them; sometimes every member of the company had one to himself. In well-furnished Viking graves horns are often found in pairs, perhaps one to be sent along each of the two rows of seats in a hall. Occasionally a single outstandingly rich horn is found, such as one Swedish one (rather earlier than the Viking Age) with a ring fixed to its mount; this may have been designed for the toasts accompanied by solemn vows, as rings were sacred objects on which oaths were sworn. Many legends and superstitions must have gathered round an object as charged with emotional associations as the drinking-horn, but few traces of these remain, apart from the sign of three interlinked horns which appears as a religious symbol on memorial stones in Gotland and Denmark.

Feasts, as has been said, lasted for several days; between the sessions of eating and drinking men amused themselves with all kinds of popular pastimes – wrestling, trials of strength, races, recitations of verse and perhaps also of stories in prose, and that dangerously provocative amusement, the organized exchange of insults (known in Scotland as 'flyting'). Any of these could lead to trouble, yet violent incidents did not necessarily spoil the general pleasure in a feast; in Valhalla itself, the worshippers of Odin could look forward to an everlasting battle in which they would for ever slay one another and for ever come to life again to take up their unending feasting:

> *All chosen champions in Odin's halls*
> *Slay each other every day;*
> *They raise the fallen and ride from the field,*
> *Sit in friendship side by side.*

Pendant showing women dancing.

9
Religious Practices and Funerary Rites

Heathen myths are probably the most widely known products of Scandinavian culture, since they had the good fortune to be recorded in the lays of the *Poetic Edda* and in the vigorous, amusing prose of Snorri Sturluson. Innumerable English adaptations have familiarized us with Thor's encounters with giants; Odin's protection of warriors, and his heavenly hall, Valhalla; Loki's guiles; the death of Balder, and the Doom of the Gods. From these tales, and other evidence, one can build up quite a detailed picture of the gods, and especially of the three major ones, Thor, Odin and Frey, who attracted most worship in the Viking Age.

The cult of Thor was the most vigorous, widespread and lasting, and was carried by the Vikings to every land they settled; an English homilist stated that Thor was the god the Danes loved most, and an Irishman calls the Norwegians of Dublin 'the tribe of Thor'. His cult grew stronger as the ninth and tenth centuries proceeded, so that when Christianity came, it was Thor who appeared the chief rival and opponent of Christ. A striking proof of this devotion is the very high proportion of personal names with the prefix 'Thor-', especially in Norway and Iceland. Many place-names in these countries also allude to him.

Thor was a sky-god, more particularly a storm-god, wielding a hammer which symbolized a thunderbolt, and, like Zeus, he was associated with oak-trees. As storm-god he was invoked by seafarers, and as sender of good or bad weather and of the fertilizing rain he was invoked by farmers (especially in Sweden). Like many other sky-gods, he was the guardian of law and justice in the community; oaths were sworn on holy rings kept in his temples, and the General Assembly of Iceland always opened on a Thursday. He also played a part in the vital ceremonies of family life and the protection of individuals; his symbol, the hammer, was used to bless a bride, a newborn child, or a funeral pyre; small hammers were widely popular as amulets; memorial stones sometimes bore formulas invoking his blessing, or else the sign of the hammer. The swastika and the axe are also thought to have been symbols of his power.

In myths he appears as a great fighter, of huge size and strength, crushing giant after giant by his hammer-blows, or struggling to slay the mighty World Serpent which his fishing-line has dragged from the ocean. In Scandinavian mythology, monstrous wolves, serpents or dragons are figures of evil and chaos, whose onslaughts threaten the ordered world of gods and men, and will at length bring it to destruction. Therefore any god or human hero who can slay a monster or bind it in chains is a powerful champion of mankind, whose exploits have religious meaning and are a fit subject for poetry or art; Thor, who outdoes all the others as an unwearying giant-killer, is the god whose power does most to guard men from forces of evil.

The character of Odin is far more complex, and its varied aspects are reflected in the many names and epithets – over 150 of them – bestowed on him by Norse poets. His chief name, Odin or Wodan, contains a valuable clue to the essence of his nature; it is related to an adjective meaning 'frenzied, mad'; similarly, Adam of Bremen, writing of Swedish heathendom in about 1070, notes briefly: 'Wodan, *id est Furor.*' It seems, from myths and legends, that three different frenzies were his gifts: that of the warrior in battle, that of the seer in a trance, and that of the poet.

As war-god, Odin wields a spear and is accompanied by carrion-eating ravens, wolves and eagles; he rejoices in rousing strife, so that under his influence men forget the holiest ties of blood or kinship, and rush to slay each other. Certain nobly-born heroes are his favourites, to whom he reveals secrets of strategy, and on whom he bestows invincible weapons; other fighters, the berserks, he inspires to such frenzy that they fight like wild beasts and, though naked, are untouched by weapons. His foes he strikes with panic, or with a kind of paralysis called the 'battle-fetter' – a power which may account for the knot shaped like a triple triangle which is believed to be a symbol of him. But a war-god's favours are capricious: sooner or later he deserts his worshipper, leaving him to be slain. For this reason Odin is the god of death, or at least of death by violence; his emissaries are the Valkyries, 'Choosers of the Slain', who grant victory to one man but summon another from the battlefield to the Otherworld. The slain are said to be 'given to Odin', and they go to Valhalla, 'Hall of the Slain', of which more will be said below; this fate was viewed ambivalently, for while most poems represent it as glorious, others are bitter that the god's reward to his worshippers should be death.

Odin is also the god of wisdom, especially the occult wisdom of seers and sorcerers; he is master of runic magic and of every sort of spell; he can call the dead from the graves and the hanged from the gallows-tree, and compel them to reveal the future; his horse Sleipnir (often said to be eight-legged) can carry men through the air or down to the Underworld; he himself is a shape-changer, whose spirit roams the world as a bird or beast while his body lies as if asleep or dead. His magic wisdom is won at the price of torments – by the loss of an eye, according to one tale; according to another, by hanging for nine days like a human sacrifice, 'himself offered to himself' (p. 151). From such myths it seems that Odin was the patron and the divine prototype of seers and magicians, especially those who (like shamans in Arctic Europe and Asia in modern times) undergo terrifying initiations and communicate with other worlds in ecstasies and mediumistic trances.

In Norse mythology, poetry is symbolized in very concrete form, as

Thor fishing for the Serpent: carved stone, Altuna, Sweden.

Bronze figurine of Thor, from Iceland.

Odin with eagle and raven;
plaque from a Vendel helmet.

sacred mead; originally it had been brewed by all the gods, but it fell into the hands of dwarves and giants, and it was Odin who rescued it from them for the use of gods and men. This view of poetic inspiration as a kind of mystic drunkenness comes rather oddly from Norse scalds, whose art was quite lacking in ecstatic quality. Probably the myth is ancient and originally referred to religious chants, in which case it would reflect Odin's role as a master of esoteric arts. Be that as it may, it was extremely popular among Norse poets, whose consequent reverence for Odin often led them to exalt him at the expense of other gods.

This exaltation of Odin is very marked in Snorri's writings; there, he is the chief of all the gods, creator of mankind, ruler of heaven and earth, who, when the end of the world draws near, will lead a band of chosen heroes to war against the forces of evil, and will die heroically in combat with a monstrous wolf. Nevertheless, it seems likely that the cult of Odin was mainly confined to special classes of men – princely rulers and the poets who served them, initiates into esoteric mysteries, members of bands of dedicated warriors – or to the special circumstances of war.

The third major god is Frey, the most prominent among a group of male and female deities concerned with peace and plenty, and with the fertility of men, animals and crops. Boars and stallions are associated with him, as symbols both of maleness and of ferocity. Njord, the god of wealth and seafaring, is his father; Freyja, the love goddess, is his twin sister, and in some sources is said to be his wife as well. The only surviving mythical tale about Frey tells of his love for Gerd, a beautiful giantess whom his messenger coaxes from the Underworld – clearly, a myth symbolizing the fertilizing of the earth by the sun's power. There exists a considerable number of thin gold foils embossed with figures of a man and woman embracing, or perhaps, in some cases, dancing; these are sometimes interpreted as showing the marriage of Frey and Gerd, though as they are found in many different regions and are often older than the Viking Age, it is unlikely that these names were always and everywhere attached to them. However, these amulets undoubtedly symbolize love, marriage and fertility, matters which in the Viking Age were particularly under the protection of Frey. He was worshipped with special fervour in Sweden; place-names incorporating his name are commonest there, and since they often refer to cornfields and meadows they show the importance of his cult in agricultural communities.

There were also groups of minor deities and spirits without individual names, known collectively as 'land spirits', 'elves', *dísir* (probably meaning 'ladies'), 'following spirits', and so forth. Fruitfulness of land and livestock, luck in hunting, fishing or farming, general prosperity and good fortune, were their spheres of activity; the 'following spirits' were attached to a family or an individual whose prosperity they ensured, whereas elves and 'land spirits' were usually associated with places rather than persons. No literary passage gives a systematic account of these rather shadowy beings; their nature and function is discovered through scattered incidental allusions, and can be confirmed by comparison with later folklore.

Bronze figurine of Frey, from Sweden.

The oldest sites for religious worship were in the open air, in holy groves and meadows, before rocks and hillocks, or on the shores of swampy lakes into which offerings were cast. Many regions of Scandinavia are rich in such place-names as Odin's Meadow, Odin's Cornfield, Thor's Crag, Thor's Grove, Frey's Cornfield, and the like. Besides places sacred to a specified god, there were many others simply called 'holy', which were probably thought of as the dwellings of gods or beneficient spirits, even if no name was given. The same must have been true of particular rocks, wells and other natural objects to which individual households brought offerings. Traces of this custom are found in several sagas and in the complaints of Christian preachers and lawgivers, for long after the conversion people still believed that 'the good spirits of the land' dwelt in groves, mounds or waterfalls, and women still gathered by caves and cairns to eat food first dedicated to them.

There are several indications that Vikings abroad practised open-air worship; those in Dublin, for instance, had a grove of huge oaks and other trees which they called 'Thor's Grove', and which was burnt by Brian Boru. In Russia too, according to the Greek Emperor Constantine Porphyrogenitus, the Swedes made offerings of birds on an island in the Dnieper 'because a giant oak-tree grows there'. Ibn Fadlan's fascinating account of a Rus merchant at prayer (p. 100) does not make it clear whether the idols and poles are set up out of doors, but the absence of any mention of a building makes this seem likely.

Sites for open-air worship in the Scandinavian homelands could be considerably more elaborate. One type of sanctuary was the *vé*, an open space marked off by some barrier such as ropes or fencing, within which the ground must not be defiled by bloodshed, nor weapons carried. A *vé* could be of great size, judging by what may perhaps be a monument of this type, erected by the Danish king Gorm the Old, who reigned at Jelling and died about 940. It consists of an artificial mound containing a double grave-chamber (perhaps for Gorm himself and his wife), to the south of which were found a number of standing stones. It has been suggested that there were originally some 200 of these, enclosing a narrow V-shaped area about 200 yards long; this the excavator interpreted as a *vé*, a sacred enclosure for public worship. However, further excavations will be needed to confirm this, since a rival theory interprets the stones as purely funerary monuments such as were sometimes set up round burial places (p. 176).

Thor's Hammer: ornate silver amulet, from Sweden.

Whether Vikings had true temples (as distinct from small shrines to shelter statues and sacred objects) is much disputed. Many written sources say that they had, but archaeological confirmation is lacking; the writers may have been misled by the constant Christian practice of worship by congregations gathered inside special buildings. Pagan methods of sacrifice (to be described below) were clearly open-air rites; but the communal feasting which often followed would be more conveniently held indoors in bad weather. Such feasts are known to have taken place at the farms of local chieftains and wealthy men; it is more likely that the ordinary main room was used for this purpose than that a special building was reserved for it. Accounts of Viking Age 'temples' in the sagas, though apparently inaccurate on this point, nevertheless give interesting details; the *Eyrbyggja Saga* thus describes a 'temple' of Thor erected by an Icelandic settler:

> It was a mighty building. There was a door in the side wall, nearer to one end of it; inside this door stood the posts of the high-seat, and in them were the nails that were called the Divine Nails. The inside was a place of great sanctuary. And right inside at the far end there was a chamber of the same form as that of a church chancel nowadays. And there in the middle of the floor stood a stand like an altar, and on this lay an arm-ring without any join, weighing twenty ounces, on which men had to swear all oaths. The chieftain had to have that ring on his arm at all public gatherings. On the stand there must also lie the bowl for the blood of sacrifice, and in it the blood-twig, like a holy-water sprinkler, with which to sprinkle from that bowl the blood, which was called *hlaut* and was the kind of blood shed when beasts were slaughtered as sacrifice to the gods. And all round that stand, the gods were set out in that holy place.

Snorri gives a description of a 'temple' at Trondheim in Norway in the tenth century, in which several of the same details occur. At the time of the feasts there, all local farmers gathered, bringing enough food and drink to last through the festival, and also cattle and horses to be sacrificed. Their blood was caught in bowls and sprinkled over all the building, outside and

in, and over all the people; the flesh was boiled in cauldrons over fires in the middle of the temple floor, and people sat round them to feast. The chieftain conducting the sacrifice consecrated the meat and drink, and the horns were passed to and fro over the fires for ceremonial drinking: the first toast to Odin, for victory and the success of the king; the second to Njord and Frey, for a good harvest and for peace; then the 'leader's toast'; the toasts to the memory of buried kinsmen.

The earliest description of a god's image is by the tenth-century traveller, Ibn Fadlan (p. 100): 'a tall upright wooden post with a face like a man's', before which the worshipper prostrated himself and laid down his offerings. The same Icelander who built the 'temple' described above had 'posts for a high-seat' carved with an image of Thor, which he had brought from Norway; it is tempting to suppose that the post itself represented the god's body, as with the idols mentioned by Ibn Fadlan, rather than that it was simply carved with a scene from Thor's life, as, say, the panelling of a hall might be.

Various passages in Snorri and in other sagas describe the appearance of more elaborate images. These too were of wood, apparently life-size, standing on pedestals or platforms, or seated in chariots. They were adorned with gold and silver, wore arm-rings, and in one instance the image of a goddess is said to have had a linen veil. The idols could be moved from the shrine; Snorri tells of a hollow statue of Thor, with his hammer in his hand, which was drawn out to the Assembly field on its platform. This particular image received daily offerings of bread and meat, and when the Christian king Olaf the Saint had it smashed, out ran snakes, toads and rats, which had grown fat on the offerings.

Later sagas give even more elaborate descriptions of Norwegian idols:

Thor sat in the middle. He was the most highly honoured. He was huge, and all adorned with gold and silver. Thor was arranged to sit in a chariot; he was very splendid. There were goats, two of them, harnessed in front of him, very well wrought. Both car and goats ran on wheels. The rope round the horns of the goats was of twisted silver, and the whole was worked with extremely fine craftsmanship.

Another late saga tells a story which, though humorous, seems to preserve genuine traditions of a cult. It appears from this that in Sweden in the late tenth century a wooden idol of Frey would be drawn in a wagon from farm to farm, accompanied by a living woman who rode beside it and was called 'the wife of Frey'. The ceremony took place in the autumn, and was intended to bless the next year's crops; the statue was welcomed with feasting when it reached a farm. This is remarkably like a ceremony practised by Danish tribes in the first century AD, in honour of the goddess Nerthus, whose symbol was drawn in a wagon through the settlements. Probably there was a long tradition of processional cults connected with various gods and goddesses; the small but intricately carved wagon found in the ninth-century Oseberg ship-burial was perhaps meant for such a ritual.

A few other details about religious ceremonies can be gleaned from scattered sources. Oracles were taken, by throwing down pieces of wood with markings on them, which were called 'sacrifice chips' or 'lot-twigs'. It seems that the cult of Frey at Uppsala involved some form of dramatic performance with clapping, 'the unmanly clatter of bells', and 'effeminate gestures'; and that in a Swedish temple of Thor there were huge, heavy bronze hammers, whose clanging imitated the noise of thunder. Naturally, ceremonies would be accompanied by chants and invocations; these may have resembled certain fragments of Icelandic poetry from the end of the tenth century, in which Thor is praised for slaughtering giants and ogresses:

> *You broke Leikn's limbs,*
> *You thrashed Thrivaldi,*
> *You struck Starkad down,*
> *You trampled on dead Gjalp.*

and:

> *Your hammer battered Keila's skull,*
> *You broke Kjallandi all to bits,*
> *You slaughtered Lut and Leidi,*
> *You drew Buseyra's blood,*
> *You harassed Hengjankjapta;*
> *Hyrrokin, she was dead before,*
> *And earlier all life was reft*
> *Full soon from swarthy Sivor.*

The most dramatic contemporary account of a heathen shrine and its cult is that given by Adam of Bremen in his *History of the Archbishops of Hamburg*, written in about 1070. Though Denmark, Norway and Iceland were by then Christian, heathendom still flourished in Sweden side by side with the new religion. Its centre was the gold-decked temple at Old Uppsala, where, according to Adam, there stood three idols: Thor enthroned in the middle, with a 'sceptre' (hammer?); on one side of him Odin, armed, and on the other a god named 'Fricco' (which must be an alternative name for Frey), who as 'the god of peace and sensual pleasures' was shown with a large phallus. Sacrifices were offered to Thor in time of danger from famine or plague, to Odin in time of war, and to 'Fricco' at the celebration of weddings.

In addition, Adam says that a major festival was held every nine years, lasting nine days, and attended by men from all over Sweden, bringing gifts. Christians who refused to attend had to buy themselves off by a fine. At this festival the sacrifice consisted of nine men and nine males each of several types of animal including dogs and horses; the blood was offered to the gods, and the bodies hung from the branches of a nearby grove, every tree of which was regarded as divine because of the rotting flesh of the victims. Adam declares that one of his informants, a Christian, had seen 72 carcasses hanging there together at one time.

Hanged men: detail from the Oseberg Tapestry.

The practice of human sacrifice had a long history among Germanic peoples. Tacitus, Jordanes, Procopius and others often refer to tribes who, at various periods from the first to the sixth century, slaughtered captives taken in battle in honour of their war-god. Several times it is mentioned that the victims, together with captured arms and other offerings, were hung up on trees; in other cases they were cast into rivers and swamps – as is confirmed by the heaps of bones and battle-gear found in Danish peat-bogs.

References to human sacrifice in the Viking Age are rarer, but still enough to confirm Adam's account of the Uppsala ceremonies; besides the valuable evidence of Arab writers (pp. 173–177), we find in one Icelandic saga the casual remark that 'heathens sacrifice the worst men, hurling them over cliffs and rocks', and in another the statement that certain criminals were 'sentenced to be sacrificed', and had their backs broken across a stone in a place sacred to Thor. Moreover there are tales of semi-legendary kings who met death in circumstances suggestive of ritual slaughter. The clearest tells of the Norwegian king Vikar, chosen by lot to be offered up to Odin; hoping to evade his fate by a mock ceremony, he stood on a stump under the thinnest branch of a fir-tree, tied to it by a noose of calf-gut round his neck, and with his most trusty follower ready to strike him with a slender reed – but the reed suddenly turned into a spear and the calf-gut into a stout rope, while the stump fell from under his feet and the branch sprang up, so that he died of stabbing and hanging simultaneously. Such a death points clearly to the cult of Odin, god of the hanged; a scene on one of the Gotland stones shows his symbol, the triple triangle, near a hanged man whom a swooping bird is about to attack, while a group of warriors hold another bird, which may also be destined to be sacrificed.

Nor are the animals hanging in the Uppsala grove unique; one Arab writer mentions the actual hanging of animals among Swedes in Russia, while others describe a related custom of stringing up a carcass on a pole – either the whole of it, as at Hedeby (p. 91), or simply the head, as among other Russian Swedes. Setting a horse's head on a pole also occurs in

A sacrifice to Odin: detail from a Gotland stone.

Icelandic sagas as a ritual for cursing or insulting an enemy. The commonest form of animal sacrifice, however, was that in which a beast was consecrated, slaughtered, and eaten at a banquet.

Nor should bloodthirsty rituals cause us to forget that other, less dramatic, ceremonies certainly formed part of daily life in farming communities. It is, for instance, obvious that ploughing, sowing and reaping must have been accompanied by appropriate rites to ensure fertility; but, to form some idea of their nature, one has to turn to accounts of folk-practices in much later centuries, such as were carried out in Sweden within living memory. At the spring ploughing, the farmer's wife would bring out to the fields some ale and a large cake, or a loaf left from the Christmas baking; the ploughman and his team would all eat part of the cake, and the rest would be crumbled and mixed into the seed to be sown. The ale would be divided into three portions, one to be drunk by the ploughman, one to be thrown over the horses, and one over the plough. The first three furrows must be cut so that the sods lay towards the sun, and earth must be rubbed on the beasts' necks or foreheads; when the work was over, all tools must be wreathed with flowers. Ceremonies of some such kind must surely have been used in Viking times, though unlike the great public feasts and sacrifices, no accounts of them have survived.

One aspect of private religious practice has left many traces, namely the use of amulets. Sagas occasionally mention men who carried small ivory or silver images of gods in their purses, and paid honour to them. Several such statuettes survive. One, found in Sweden, shows a naked squatting figure, wearing an arm-ring, and with phallus erect; because of this last feature, it is almost certainly Frey. Another, found in Iceland, is undoubtedly Thor, seated on a throne and clasping a curious hammer. Both these are bronze, and in both the god wears a conical cap and has a strongly marked moustache and beard. There is also a bone figurine from Lund, with no distinctive feature to show which god it is; and a strange Norwegian image of an animal seated on a throne, which may also be an amulet. It is also worth noting that the squatting figurine found among playing-pieces in an Icelandic grave clasps its beard with the same gesture as the religious statuettes; perhaps, therefore, it belongs with these and was only accidentally associated with playing-pieces. The figurines of women holding drinking horns, men in horned helmets, and men on horseback are other probable examples of religious amulets and luck-bringing talismans.

By far the most popular amulet was the hammer of Thor. More than 40 have been found, mostly dating from the later tenth or early eleventh century; they usually have a loop to hang by, and sometimes a chain or ring as well. They vary in size from less than an inch to nearly three inches, and in richness from the simplest undecorated iron to finely worked silver or

Figurines of men and women, possible amulets; from Sweden.

bronze, elaborated with a bird-like head. Both men and women wore them, for they are found in the graves of both; even more frequently they are found on the sites of houses or buried with a hoard of treasure, possibly as a magic safeguard against thieves.

It may be that their popularity was stimulated by the Christian custom of wearing miniature crosses. Certainly a market for both existed side by side, for a metal-worker's mould found in Jutland was prepared for casting both hammers and crosses. Again, there is a bronze object from Iceland which, if worn hanging from the animal head at one end, would seem to be a form of hammer, while the other way up it would resemble a cross; moreover, a cross-shaped hole has been cut in it. One is reminded of the outlook of the Icelander Helgi the Lean, a man of mixed beliefs who, though a Christian, still called on Thor at sea and in matters of great difficulty.

Individual Scandinavians might have a warmer personal devotion to one god than to another, but when men gathered for communal worship and feasting, many gods were honoured side by side. The upkeep of the main temple in a district was the responsibility of the local chieftain, supported by contributions from the other households; it seems always to have been the chieftain (or king) who presided at sacrifices and religious feasts, at least in Norway and Iceland. In Sweden, on the other hand, there may have been a class of professional officiants, for Adam of Bremen speaks of 'priests' at the temple of Uppsala; it is indeed only natural to suppose that such a large-scale cult as he describes would need the services of full-time priests. Similarly, Ibn Rustah's account of Swedish traders in Russia includes a reference to a professional priesthood:

> They have their *attiba* [wizards], who have as much authority over their goods as if they were their masters, for they order them to make offerings of women, men, and cattle, just as they choose. When these wizards have chosen what they want, it is impossible to evade their demands; the wizard takes the human being or animal away, ties a rope round its neck, and hangs it from a pole till it expires, saying 'this is an offering to God'.

Denmark, too, had heathen priests, whose office was recorded on their memorials; clearest of these is a stone from Snoldelev bearing religious symbols (swastika and interlaced drinking-horns), and inscribed: 'Gunvald's stone, son of Roald, *thul* in Salhaug'. The term *thul* occurs elsewhere too; it may mean 'soothsayer' or 'reciter of incantations'.

At a lower level, there were individuals who made a livelihood by the exercise of magic powers. The sagas have many tales of men or women being employed to undertake various magical and divinatory rites, from the finding of lost objects or forecasting the season's crops, to black magic and storm-raising. Many of these stories must be sheer fiction, but others, by their more authentic air, seem based on real practices. Very often the wizard or seer is said to be a 'Finn', i.e. one of the Lappish race that were the aboriginal inhabitants of northern Scandinavia, and it is likely that some of these made a living in this way among their Norse neighbours.

Icelandic amulet combining the Hammer, a monster-head, and the Cross.

Among such persons was one type of female seer known as a *vǫlva*; the term occurs in both poetry and prose, and the women to whom it applies are not said to be 'Finns', but Norse. Several sagas tell how they travelled from farm to farm, sometimes in groups, to answer questions about the future. Before giving her replies the *vǫlva* would go into a trance, sometimes sitting on a high platform, and accompanied by chants and incantations by her assistants. The fullest account of such a seance comes from *The Saga of Eirik the Red*, a work of the late thirteenth century describing events in the Greenland settlement at the beginning of the eleventh. The episode may, in its context, be fiction; but the author's account clearly shows that he must have known a great deal about such procedures. Perhaps his knowledge came, directly or indirectly, from observing the shamanistic rites of Lapps in northern Norway.

He says that there was a woman in the Greenland settlement, a *vǫlva*, who used to go round the farms in winter to answer questions about the coming season, or about men's destinies; she was welcomed with feasts. One bad season, she was invited to a certain house, where a high-seat with a cushion of hen's feathers was prepared for her:

> She was wearing a blue strapped cloak, all set with stones down to the hem; she had glass beads round her neck, and on her head a black lambskin hood with a lining of white catskin; and in her hand she had a staff with a knob on it, which was mounted with brass and had stones set in it round the base of the knob. She had a belt of touchwood round her, and on it was a large skin pouch in which she kept her charms which she had to have for her magic. She had hairy calfskin shoes on her feet, and long shoelaces with big tin knobs on the ends; she had on her hands gloves of catskin, white inside, and hairy.

She was respectfully greeted, and asked to 'run her eyes over household, herd and homestead'. Her food was specially made, being porridge with the milk of goats' beestings, and a dish of hearts of every species of animal available. Next day, while preparing to work her spells, she demanded to have as helper some woman who would know how to recite certain chants to summon the spirits; one was found, with some difficulty. The *vǫlva* mounted a platform, round which women formed a ring, and the seance began. When the chants ended, she uttered prophecies of good fortune, answered questions, and then departed to another farm.

Woman with ceremonial staff.

In this description, the platform, the chanting, the summoning of spirits, and the elaborate costume with animal skins are all reminiscent of the rituals of shamans, while the ornate knobbed staff appears on certain Danish gold-foil figures as early as the sixth century. Such magic practices (and others more sinister, at which the sources merely hint) were in some way linked with the cults of Freyja and Odin, both of whom are said to have practised magic themselves.

To draw general conclusions on Viking beliefs about death and their treatment of the dead is a very complex task, whether one approaches the matter through archaeological or through literary evidence. Actual practices varied greatly; even the most widespread rite, that of equipping the dead with his personal possessions, was not universal; it was the regular practice of Swedes and Norwegians, but was far rarer among Danes.

The two basic rites were burial and cremation, but in each case many variants were possible. Graves have been found occurring singly, or in small groups, or again in large cemeteries on the outskirts of towns; in Christian countries, Vikings sometimes chose burial in churchyards but can be recognized by their grave-goods. In burial, the corpse was most commonly laid directly in the ground, in a naturally flexed position, and it is sometimes possible to infer that it was covered with a cloak or supported by pillows. It would be wearing normal clothing and jewellery, and its weapons, tools and various other goods would be arranged round it. Often the grave would be left unmarked, but in other cases it might be covered by a cairn or by an earth mound, or again it might be surrounded with stones set in a circle, square or triangle, or in the shape of a ship. The body might, on the other hand, be put in a coffin, with few if any goods; this was common in the town graveyards of Birka and Hedeby, where it may have been spread by foreign influences. More elaborate was a method popular among the wealthier Swedes, and usually reserved for men; here a stout wooden chamber was built to house the corpse, and it was furnished with many of the dead man's possessions; often, the bodies of horses and dogs were laid in it, near the

Graves shaped like ships with stone settings, at Hjarnø, Jutland.

entrance. The Swedes took the custom with them to their Russian settlements; it must be to this that Ibn Rustah refers when he says of the Rus:

> When a great man among them dies, they make a grave like a large house and place him in it. With him they lay his clothes, the gold arm-rings he wore, and also much food, and bowls of drink, and coins. They also lay his favourite wife in the grave with him, while she is still alive. Then the door of the grave is blocked up, and she dies there.

The last detail, sensational though it may seem, is partially confirmed by the finding of a chamber-grave at Birka which contained the bodies of two women, one properly laid out, but the other lying in a twisted position; this suggests that the latter had been buried alive, perhaps as a slave with her mistress. Only slightly less remarkable was the custom of killing a slave, usually a woman, to be buried or burnt with the master, as is described in detail by Ibn Fadlan among the Swedes of Russia (p. 182). There are occasional hints of the same thing in Icelandic lays and sagas, and also of suttee, the killing of a wife to accompany her husband in death. However, these customs can never have been so common in the Scandinavian homelands as the Arabs say they were in Russia, or they would have left more traces in the archaeological record; probably the fact that the Rus slave-traders had so many women readily available made it cheaper for them to indulge in practices which were rare luxuries elsewhere.

It may be for the same economic reason that examples of human sacrifice also occur in some of the western Viking settlements, where slaves were common. Two have been found on the Isle of Man, one at Balladoole and the other at Ballateare; the former is a boat-burial with two skeletons of which one is probably female, and in the latter case the skeleton of a young woman with her skull smashed lay in the earth of a ninth-century burial mound, a few feet above a coffin containing a man's skeleton. Similarly at Westness in the Orkneys a 50-year-old woman seems to have been slaughtered on top of the already buried body of a younger warrior. In Scandinavia itself only three possible instances have so far been discovered: the Oseberg ship-burial, the grave at Birka described above, and another ship-burial at Valsgarde.

The most picturesque form of burial was that in which the corpse was laid inside a ship and lavishly supplied with food, weapons, tools, and household gear, together with the ship's full equipment; animals would be sacrificed (especially dogs and horses) and their bodies laid nearby; finally the whole thing would be carefully buried, either under a mound or in a pit below ground-level. This custom is first found in Sweden, starting before the Viking period, and confined to certain very wealthy families. At Vendel and at Valsgärde there are whole series of such burials, spanning the centuries from about 600 to 1000 or 1100. Here, generation after generation, the head of the family was interred in exactly the same manner – sitting or lying in the ship's stern, facing a pile of goods heaped in the bow, and with his weapons

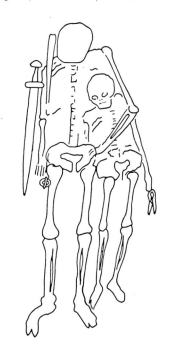

Man and woman in one Viking grave, at Stestovitsi, Russia.

by his side or actually in his grasp; slaughtered horses and dogs were lined up in pairs inside or outside the ship. This remarkable conservatism is the more striking in that cremation was the normal rite in this district in the earlier part of the period, while later Christianity was powerful there; clearly, tradition was very strong in these two families.

Norway too had rich princely ship-burials, notably at Gokstad and Oseberg, where the corpse lay in bed in a small wooden tent-like structure on the after-deck; there was a profusion of goods and equipment of every sort, and the bodies of many horses and dogs lay round the ships. At Tune the ceremony was part cremation, part burial; the man's body is represented only by charred bones, but the ship is unburnt. But in Norway, unlike Sweden, the fashion for ship-burials spread rapidly among all social levels during the Viking Age; over 1,000 have been found, both at home and in the settlements, though of course in many cases the 'ship' is only a small boat. The timbers have almost always rotted, but rows of rusty clinch-nails prove that a boat was there.

Finally, it is worth mentioning one unique burial at Fyrkat camp, where the body, that of a woman, had been laid to rest in a wagon; it provides a curious parallel to a passage in the *Poetic Edda* telling how Brynhild was laid in a covered wagon to be burnt on the pyre, and how afterwards she drove this wagon down the road to the Underworld.

The other major funeral rite was cremation, which Snorri says was characteristic of Odin's worshippers:

> Odin made it a law that all dead men should be burnt, and their belongings laid with them on the pyre, and the ashes cast into the sea or buried in the ground. He said that in this way every man would come to Valhalla with whatever riches had been laid with him on the pyre. . . . Outstanding men should have a mound raised to their memory, and all others famous for manly deeds should have a memorial stone. . . . It was their belief that the higher the smoke rose in the air, the higher would be raised the man whose pyre it was, and the more goods were burnt with him, the richer he would be.

Cremations are found all over the Scandinavian lands. Normally the burning took place on a different site from that where the ashes were to rest, and when the fire had died down all the smaller debris – charred bones of man and beast, charcoal, ashes, and burnt fragments of metalwork – were brought there and spread in a neat layer over a yard or two of ground. Bigger objects, such as swords, axe-blades or shield-bosses, might be piled in the centre, sometimes in or under a cauldron; occasionally they were deliberately damaged by bending them while they were still red-hot. Then the remains would be covered with a layer of soil, over which a cairn or a mound might or might not be raised. As with burials, the amount of goods and animals sacrificed varied widely. In some cremations one finds many ship's clinch-nails among the debris, and though this might sometimes be merely the result of using old timbers as fuel, in the wealthier cremations it is practically certain that the dead man's ship was itself the centre of the pyre, so that it is possible to speak of ship-cremations as a parallel to ship-burials.

Finally, there are literary accounts of a rite, rare but impressive, in which the pyre was built on board a ship which was then set drifting out to sea, blazing as it went; the god Balder is said to have been cremated in this way, and also two very early kings, Haki of Norway and Sigurd Ring of Sweden, who lived (if they are not purely legendary) before the real Viking Age. It is wrong to assume that this was the typical funeral of Viking chieftains.

Behind these varied customs lie two basic conceptions of the afterlife – that the dead will 'live' in their graves as in a home, or that they are 'sent

Excavation of a Viking Age ship burial.

forth' on their journey to the Otherworld. Cremation seems to fit more naturally with the latter view (and Snorri apparently interpreted it in this way), while burials, especially those in chamber-graves and those where the dead are laid on beds, fit better with the former. The chief problem concerns the ships and horses; were these merely included as cherished possessions of the dead man, or were they thought of as his means of transport to the Otherworld? It has been argued that the latter can be ruled out because in some cases the boat is placed upside down *over* the body, or is moored to, or weighed down by, a boulder; and that there are no clear references in Norse literature to the realm of the dead being reached by water, though there are several to dead men riding or walking to Valhalla. On the other hand, the normal position of the ship does inevitably suggest sailing, and the idea of a 'Ship of the Dead' is so ancient and widespread that it would be almost incredible if it played no part in the beliefs of a seafaring people such as the Scandinavians.

Turning to literature, one finds the same duality. Most sagas present the dead as 'living' in their burial-mounds, or, occasionally, inside a holy mountain; they are surrounded by treasures and weapons, and will rise to fight intruders. Evil men may leave their graves by night and roam about, killing men and cattle, till their animated corpses are laid by beheading or burning; the benevolent dead, on the other hand, can bring help and luck to the living. By contrast, the myths and poems lay far more stress on distant Otherworlds – the dark realm of the goddess Hel, and Odin's paradise, Valhalla. This last was pictured as a vast hall to which noble warriors, Odin's favourites, would be welcomed by Valkyries and the heroes of ancient legend, and where they would feast till the end of the world. The concept is finely expressed in three tenth-century poems, lays in memory of kings of Norway; that on Eirik Bloody-Axe (d. 954) begins with Odin foreseeing the arrival of a worthy guest:

> *'What dream was this,' said Odin, 'for I thought I*
> *rose ere day*
> *To clear space in Valhalla for an army of the slain?*
> *I aroused my chosen champions, I bade them all rise up,*
> *To spread rugs on the benches, scour goblets for the*
> *board;*
> *I bade Valkyries proffer wine, as if a prince were*
> *come.'*

Scenes on the Gotland picture-stones may embody the same idea. Two of them show on their upper panels a man on an eight-legged horse approaching a domed house, and being welcomed by a woman who offers a drinking-horn; this (unless it is a scene from a lost myth about Odin himself) must surely be a dead warrior riding to Valhalla on Odin's horse Sleipnir, and being greeted by a Valkyrie. Another bears pictures which may, though less certainly, be interpreted as a funerary scene; first there is a battle, with eagles preying on the dying; then a group of warriors with swords reversed (in mourning?), and an eight-legged horse with a body stretched above it, presumably Sleipnir carrying a corpse; and thirdly, a triumphant procession, which may represent the same man's arrival in the Otherworld. As so often, the problem is to know on which level to interpret the pictures: as religious symbolism, legendary narrative, or an incident from real life. The same question arises over the ships so often shown on these stones, which might be Ships of the Dead, or simply an indication that the man commemorated was a seafarer. However, the woman proferring drink to a rider recurs so often, not only on the picture-stones, but as a metal figurine, that she must have religious meaning; of the mythological women known to us, the welcoming Valkyrie is by far the likeliest to be represented in this way.

We are fortunate in having a vivid first-hand account of a Viking funeral, thanks to the Arab traveller Ibn Fadlan, who was curious about such matters, and described the ceremonies he witnessed on the death of a Swedish chieftain in the Volga region in about 922. There are striking similarities between his story and what is known from archaeology and literature, and also a mass of detail that could be known in no other way.

He begins by stressing that a funeral such as he saw is only for the rich; poor men are simply burnt in a small boat, but a rich man's wealth is split in three parts – one for the heirs, one to provide clothes (and presumably other equipment too) for the corpse, and one to buy ale for the funeral feast. It takes ten days to prepare the clothes and all that is needed, and during this

The warrior's arrival at Valhalla: top panel of a Gotland stone.

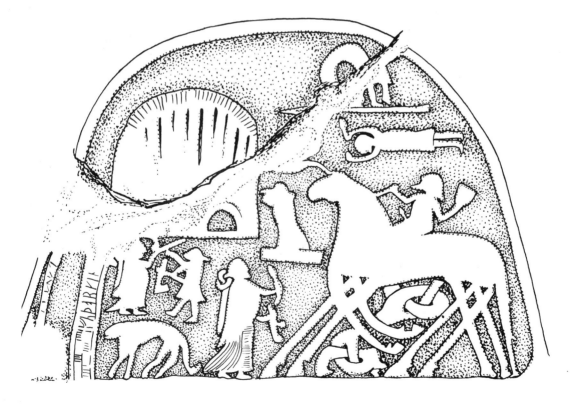

time the body lies in a temporary grave, with food and drink and a musical instrument beside it; in connection with this grave Ibn Fadlan mentions not merely earth but 'woodwork', so it may have been something like the wooden chamber-graves mentioned above. He later states that the body had been embalmed, but that 'owing to the coldness of the ground' it had turned black by the time it was dug up again, though even so it did not smell. Meanwhile, there is another custom to be followed:

> When a chieftain dies, his family say to his slave-girls and servants: 'Which of you will die with him?' Then one of them says: 'I will.' When this person has said this, he is forced to do it and is not free to retract; even if he wanted to, it would not be allowed. It is mostly the slave-girls who do this. So, when the man I am speaking of died, they said to his slave-girls: 'Which of you will die with him?', and one of them said: 'I will.'

From that moment the girl was never left alone; two other slave-girls waited on her constantly, and she herself 'drank and sang joyfully every day, and seemed to be looking forward to a coming happiness'.

Meanwhile, Ibn Fadlan watched the preparation of the actual pyre. The dead man's ship had been dragged ashore from the river, propped up with stakes, and surrounded with 'something that looked like a great stack of wood', on top of which it rested. There was a tent pitched on the deck of the ship, and men brought a bench to set in it, and covered this bench with rugs and cushions of brocaded Byzantine silk, under the guidance of 'an old woman whom they called the Angel of Death', whom Ibn Fadlan describes as 'an old, hag-like woman, thick-set and grim-looking'. This tent and the couch inside it find their exact parallels in the Gokstad and Oseberg ship-burials where the corpse lies in a bed inside a little wooden shelter very like a tent.

So, when all was at length ready, the dead man was removed from his temporary grave, stripped of the clothes he had died in, and re-clothed in specially made garments of rich silk, trimmed with gold buttons and sable fur. The corpse was carried on board ship and into the tent, where it was laid on the rugs and propped up on the cushions.

> Then they brought ale, fruit and sweet-smelling plants and laid them by him; they also brought bread, meat and leeks and threw them in front of him. Then they brought a dog, cut it in two, and threw it into the ship. Next, they brought all his weapons and laid them beside him. Then they took two horses and made them gallop round till they sweated, whereupon they cut them in pieces with swords and threw their flesh into the ship. In the same way they brought two cows, and these too they cut to pieces and threw into the ship. Then they brought a cock and hen, killed them, and threw them in. Meanwhile, the slave-girl who had chosen to be killed was walking to and fro; she would go inside one or other of their tents, and the owner of the tent would make love with her, saying: 'Tell your master I did this only for love of him.'

This girl now played the central part in a very curious symbolic ceremony. Some men led her to 'a thing like a door-frame which they had made'; she seated herself on the palms of their hands, and three times they lifted her high enough for her to look over the top of the 'door-frame', and each time she said something. Then they handed her a hen; she cut off the head and threw it away, and threw the body of the hen into the ship. Ibn Fadlan asked his interpreter to explain this:

> He replied: 'The first time they lifted her up she said: "Look, I see my father and mother!" The second time she said: "Look, I see all my dead kinsmen sitting there!" The third time she said: "Look, I see my master sitting in Paradise! Paradise is green and fair, and there are men and young lads with him. He is calling me, let me go to him!"'

Clearly, the wooden frame symbolizes a barrier between this world and the Otherworld; the girl, herself about to die, can see the paradise beyond it. The killing of the hen, which here seems almost casual, becomes more significant in view of the fact that cocks and hens are frequently found as offerings in graves, and in view of a strange story told by the Danish historian Saxo about a legendary hero named Hadding. This hero was led through the Otherworld by a mysterious woman, who brought him at last to a high wall which barred their path; there she produced a cock, wrung its head off, and threw the head and the body over the wall. Immediately the cock came to life and crowed. This legend and the ritual enacted by the girl must surely be connected; taken together, they form a vivid symbol of the renewed life beyond the barrier of death.

After the ceremony, the girl was handed over to the old woman called the Angel of Death and her two daughters; the girl gave her arm-rings and ankle-rings to these women. They led her up on to the ship, but did not let her go into the tent.

> Then some men came who had shields and sticks, and they handed her a beaker of liquor; she sang over it and drank it up. The interpreter told me: 'Now with this she is bidding farewell to all her friends.' Next, another beaker was handed to her; she took it, and made her singing long drawn out; but the old woman hurried her, to make her drink it up and go into the tent where her master was. I was watching her, and she looked quite dazed; she tried to go into the tent, but stuck her head between it and the ship's side. Then the old woman took hold of her hand and managed to get her into the tent, and the old woman herself went inside with her. The men then began to beat their shields with sticks so that no sound of her shrieking should be heard, for fear other girls should become frightened and not want to seek to die with their masters. Then six men went into the tent, and all made love with her. After this they laid her beside her dead master; two held her legs and two her hands, and the woman called the Angel of Death wound a cord with knotted ends round her neck, passing the ends out on either side and handing them to the last two men to pull.

Then she stepped forward with a broad-bladed dagger, and began to drive it in and pluck it out again between the girl's ribs, while the two men choked her with the cord, and so she died.

After this, whoever was the closest kinsman of the dead man came forward. He took a wooden stick and set light to it; then he walked backwards, with his back to the ship and his face to the people, holding the stick in one hand and with the other hand laid on his backside; he was naked. By this means, the wood they had put just under the ship was set on fire, immediately after they had laid the slave-girl they had killed beside her master. Then the people came forward with wood and timber; each brought a stick with its tip on fire and threw it on the wood lying under the ship, so that the flames took hold, first on the wood, and then on the ship, and then on the tent and the man and the woman and everything inside the ship. Thereupon a strong, fierce wind arose, so that the flames grew stronger and the fire blazed even more.

A man of the Rus was standing beside me, and I heard him talking to the interpreter, who was near him. I asked him what he had said to him, and he answered: 'He said: "You Arabs are stupid." I asked: "Why so?" He answered: "Why, because you take the people you most love and honour and throw them into the ground, and the earth and creeping creatures and growing things destroy them. We, on the other hand, burn

A twelfth-century church, Borgund, Norway; the steep roofs and monster-heads may derive from pre-Christian shrines.

them in an instant, so that they go to Paradise in that very hour." Then he gave a roar of laughter, and when I asked him about this, he replied: "For the love of him, his Lord has sent this wind to carry him away at the right time!"' And, in fact, not much time passed before the ship and the timber and the slave-girl and her master had all turned into ashes and so into dust.

It is obviously an Odin-worshipper whom we hear speaking; his belief in the power of fire to bear the dead to Valhalla is exactly that which Snorri mentions. The method by which the girl is killed is very like that of a sacrifice to Odin, where hanging and stabbing with a spear were combined; the differences might be due to the sex of the victim. Strangest of all is the figure of the old hag, 'called the Angel of Death', who apparently directs much of the ritual, and slays the chief victim with her own hands – for her title is quite a passable paraphrase of 'Valkyrie', 'Chooser of the Slain'. It may be sheer coincidence, but on the other hand it may mean that in the cult of Odin there were human priestesses who used the same title as the supernatural warrior-goddesses who were his messengers. In this and other matters (e.g. ritual nakedness as a sign of mourning, and the sexual elements in the ceremonies), Ibn Fadlan's direct and dispassionate narrative has preserved details of archaic religious behaviour whose existence could hardly be suspected from the Scandinavian traditions in the form in which they have reached us, modified either by poetic or by Christian influences.

He concludes his story by describing the making of the mound. As archaeology also shows, this was not erected on the site of the actual pyre; he unfortunately does not say whether the ashes were laid in it, but it is reasonable to suppose that they were, though the raising of empty mounds as pure cenotaphs is also sometimes known in Scandinavia. The final act of the mourners, the setting up of an inscribed wooden post, is a forerunner of the custom of setting up memorial stones, later so popular among the Swedes; here it is placed on the mound itself, as a last tribute to a Viking chieftain:

After this, on the spot where the ship had first lain when they dragged it up from the river, they built something that looked like a round mound. In the middle of it they set up a big post of birch wood, on which they wrote the name of this man and the name of the king of the Rus; then they went on their way.

Suggestions for further reading

ALMGREN, B. *The Viking* 1966
ARBMAN, H. *The Vikings* 1961
BRØGGER, A.W. and SHETELIG, H. *The Viking Ships* 1951
BRØNDSTED, J. *The Vikings* Penguin Books, revised translation 1965
DAVIDSON, H.R.E. *Gods and Myths of Northern Europe* Penguin Books 1964
DAVIDSON, H.R.E. *Pagan Scandinavia* 1967
DAVIDSON, H.R.E. *The Sword in Anglo-Saxon England* 1962
FOOTE, P.G. and WILSON, D.M. *The Viking Achievement* 1971
HAMILTON, J.R.C. *Excavations at Jarlshof, Shetland* 1956
JANSSON, S.B.F. *The Runes of Sweden* 1962
JONES, G. *A History of the Vikings* 1968
JONES, G. *The Norse Atlantic Saga* 1964
KENDRICK, T.D. *A History of the Vikings* 1930
KROGH, K.J. *Viking Greenland* 1967
LOYN, H.R. *The Vikings in Britain* 1977
MAGNUSSON, M. *The Viking Expansion Westwards* 1973
McGRAIL, S. and McKEE, E. *The Gokstad Faering: The Building and Trials of the Replica of an Ancient Boat* 1974
NØRLUND, P. *Viking Settlers in Greenland* 1936
OXENSTIERNA, E. *The Norsemen* 1966
OXENSTIERNA, E. *The World of the Norsemen* 1967
SAWYER, P.H. *The Age of the Vikings* 1962
SHETELIG, H., ed. *Viking Antiquities in Great Britain and Ireland* 1940, 1954, 6 vols
SHETELIG, H. and FALK, H., transl. GORDON, E.V. *Scandinavian Archaeology* 1937
STENTON, F.M. *Anglo-Saxon England* 1947
TURVILLE-PETRE, E.O.G. *Myth and Religion of the North* 1964
VERDANSKY, G. *The Origins of Russia* 1959
WILSON, D.M. *Civil and Military Engineering in Viking Age Scandinavia* 1978
WILSON, D.M. and KLINDT-JENSEN, O. *Viking Art* 1966
WILSON, D.M. *The Vikings and their Origins* 1970

Most of the Icelandic sagas have been several times translated; new translations or recent re-editions of old translations of sagas referred to in the course of this book include:
Egil's Saga, Gwyn Jones 1960
The Saga of Eirik the Red and Other Icelandic Sagas, Gwyn Jones 1961; The World's Classics Series. *Eirik's Saga* is also included in the same author's *The Norse Atlantic Saga*, and in *The Vinland Sagas* transl. Magnus Magnusson and Hermann Pálsson 1965; Penguin Books
Eyrbyggja Saga, Paul Schach 1959

The Saga of Gisli, George Johnston 1963

The Saga of the Greenlanders. This is included in Gwyn Jones *The Norse Atlantic Saga* and in Magnusson and Pálsson *The Vinland Sagas*

The Saga of Grettir the Strong, George Hight 1914, Everyman's Library; revised reprint 1965

Heimskrinla, by Snorri Sturluson, transl. Samuel Laing 1914, 1930, Everyman's Library, 2 vols; revised reprint 1961, 1964, 3 vols

The Saga of the Jomsvikings, N.F. Blake 1962

Njal's Saga, Magnus Magnusson and Hermann Pálsson 1960, Penguin Books. Also *The Saga of Burnt Njal*, George Dasent 1911, Everyman's Library; revised reprint 1957

Two other Icelandic works several times referred to are *The Poetic Edda* transl. H.A. Bellows 1923, and Snorri Sturluson's collection of myths, *The Prose Edda*, the most important sections of which have been translated by J.I. Young 1954

Index